THE
STUDENT'S SURVIVAL GUIDE
TO RESEARCH

ALA Neal-Schuman purchases fund advocacy, awareness, and accreditation programs for library professionals worldwide.

the STUDENT'S

SURVIVAL

GUIDE  to

RESEARCH

Monty L. McAdoo

Neal-Schuman

An imprint of the American Library Association

Chicago 2015

Monty L. McAdoo has a bachelor's degree in psychology, an MA in student personnel services, a second master's degree in library science, and a DEd degree in administration and leadership studies. He is the author of *Fundamentals of Library Instruction* and *Building Bridges: Connecting Faculty, Students, and the College Library* (both from ALA Editions). He has more than twenty years of experience as a professional librarian and currently serves as research and instruction librarian at Edinboro University of Pennsylvania. In addition to providing traditional library user education, Dr. McAdoo has developed and teaches an undergraduate class on information ethics and has also taught graduate-level courses in both counseling and research.

. . . .

© 2015 by the American Library Association

Extensive effort has gone into ensuring the reliability of the information in this book; however, the publisher makes no warranty, express or implied, with respect to the material contained herein.

ISBN: 978-0-8389-1276-8 (paper)

Library of Congress Cataloging-in-Publication Data
McAdoo, Monty L., author.
  The student's survival guide to research / Monty L. McAdoo.
    pages cm
  Includes bibliographical references and index.
  ISBN 978-0-8389-1276-8
  1. Research—Handbooks, manuals, etc. 2. Information retrieval—Handbooks, manuals, etc. 3. Report writing—Handbooks, manuals, etc. I. Title.
  ZA3075.M43 2015
  001.4—dc23
                                    2015011082

Cover design by Kirstin Krutsch.
Text design and composition in the Adobe Caslon Pro and Whitney typefaces by Ryan Scheife / Mayfly Design.

♾ This paper meets the requirements of ANSI/NISO Z39.48–1992 (Permanence of Paper).

Printed in the United States of America
19 18 17 16 15   5 4 3 2 1

To Pat…
teacher, mentor, colleague, friend,
and so much more

CONTENTS

FIGURES

INTRODUCTION

Research can be challenging.

You probably don't want to hear that, but it's true. Increasingly, the sheer amount of information available can be intimidating to even the most experienced of researchers. That the number and variety of search tools used to sift through this information continue to grow only makes matters worse. In turn, the strategies and methods for conducting efficient and effective research continue to grow as well. These and other factors certainly contribute to the challenges of research.

Beginning researchers as well as those who don't often do research face their own, additional, unique set of challenges. For example, many don't understand or aren't familiar with the research process. Some have no idea which search tools to use or even how to get started using them—let alone using them effectively. Others underestimate the amount of time it takes to successfully conduct research or otherwise have difficulty managing their time throughout the research process. Add to that other coursework and various other considerations, and, well . . .

Sound familiar? If so, this book is for you!

So . . . yes . . . research is a challenge. Everyone—even the veteran researcher—encounters difficulties at some point. But, rest assured, these obstacles are not insurmountable. With that in mind and as you begin to use this book, it might be helpful to think of research as a foreign language. The words might not make sense at first. You might not understand what's being said or how to apply the rules of the language of research to your particular assignment.

That said, this book will not make you an expert researcher nor meet all your research needs. (You probably don't want to hear that either.) But, truth be told, no matter how well this book is written, no matter how much detail is provided, no matter how much you absorb, you will not become an expert researcher after reading this book. In fact, there is no trick, no short-cut, no quick fix to becoming a good researcher.

As with any skill, to become more fluent, to become a better researcher, requires time, patience, and lots of practice. No one walks into a language class and becomes fluent the first day or after just one lesson. You might start off by learning basic pronunciation. Over time, as your vocabulary and your knowledge of how to speak and write the language grow, your comfort with the language will grow as well.

The same is true of research. The more you do it, the more experience you have with it, the easier it will become and the better you are likely to become at it.

In that context—and sticking with the research-as-foreign-language metaphor—think of this book as a sort of travel dictionary. It is not designed to be exhaustive, providing you with every possible word you might encounter. Rather, it is intended to provide you with a working knowledge of the language. Armed with the key terms you are most likely to encounter, you will travel through the land of research much more smoothly.

Although the chapters can be read independently, it is recommended that you read them in the order in which they are presented. By reading chapters out of sequence, you risk losing the flow of the content—how the concepts and strategies presented relate to and with one another. The reflections that appear at the end of each chapter are not so much practice exercises as they are thought exercises, designed to help you think more critically about yourself and the research process. Words highlighted throughout the text appear in the glossary at the end.

Bon voyage!

CHAPTER 1

What Is Research?

. . . .

By enrolling in a class requiring **research**, you've essentially made (or been forced to make) the decision to conduct research. But what does that mean? Effective research involves a lot of time, energy, and effort. For those and other reasons, research can be a daunting experience, particularly for beginning researchers and for students who don't conduct research very often.

But feeling overwhelmed is okay. As with any task that you do for the first time or that you don't do often, some degree of hesitation, stress, and uncertainty is expected. Given the vast amount of information and resources available to today's researcher, the research process can be intimidating even for veteran researchers.

Defining Research
. . . .

Individuals conduct research for many reasons. Despite this fact, when people hear the term, one of two images typically comes to mind. Some envision a scientist in a lab coat performing experiments. Others imagine a college student sitting in the **library** reading and taking notes. (For the purposes of this book, it is this second example you should think of when the term *research* is used.)

Whatever form it takes, all research shares several key characteristics as outlined in figure 1.1. The goals of each researcher and the techniques each employs may appear dramatically different. However, every researcher is attempting to address a specific information need. In that respect, a scientist trying to find a cure for a disease is no different from a student like you

1

who has been asked to write a **research paper** on Shakespeare: you're both trying to find information for a specific purpose. For this reason, it should come as no surprise that research is often equated with learning.

Characteristics of Research

All research...

Involves acquiring, interpreting, and assimilating information

Organizes and presents information via a narrative, a presentation, or both (*examples*: journal article, term paper, conference presentation, lecture)

Is systematic and organized

Provides a description, explanation, or understanding of a particular topic, idea, or problem

Focuses on the discovery or interpretation of facts

Addresses a specific information need

Is cyclical in that it starts and ends with a problem or question

Why Do Research?

If you haven't already discovered this, in college your instructors are not going to simply give you information. You need to find it on your own. However, no lecture, article, book, or website—or any other source of information—can cover every aspect of a single topic. You may need to consult multiple sources in multiple formats before you have a good understanding of a particular topic or idea. You may need to decide between two contradictory sources of information—for example, what was true ten years ago may no longer be.

The many reasons to conduct research include these:

- You will be able to pursue your own interests and ideas.
- You will be able to effect a change in yourself, others, and society using the information you acquire.

- You will discover effective and efficient ways to access and acquire information.
- Your ability to think critically about information and its sources will increase.
- Your ability to synthesize, organize, and present information in a meaningful way will increase.
- You can determine gaps in your knowledge and understanding of a topic.

"Why Can't I Just Use the Internet?"

Many beginning researchers ask this question. Searching the Internet has become commonplace. It is no longer a mysterious science understood only by techies and computer nerds. Most students have grown up with the Internet. Moreover, although one may have to sift through some trash to find the treasure, most individuals are generally able to find something of relevance. The near-instant results also provide immediate gratification.

Most beginning researchers do not have this same level of comfort or degree of success searching for books and articles. They often don't know which **search tool** to use to do so. In some cases, they are not even aware that such search tools exist. The variability in **interfaces** and search tool features makes it difficult to know how to conduct a search. Acquiring the content they want may require more time and involve additional steps, such as photocopying or requesting material from another library.

So ... back to your question: "Why can't I just use the Internet?"

Although more and more information is being digitized all the time, a significant amount of information is still available only in printed format. This is especially true for many scholarly or academic sources of information—the types of sources most professors will expect you to be using. Your library's information resources are often the only way to access these sources directly and free of charge.

In addition, you simply might not be permitted to use Internet sources. Because a lot of information found on the Internet is inaccurate or misleading, some instructors won't allow you to use more than a limited number of websites (if any) as sources.

In the end, the answer to the question requires you to examine the function of the Internet itself. In doing so, keep in mind that, just like books and articles, Internet-based information is ultimately just one more tool in your information toolbox. That is, some tools work better for some jobs than for others. For example, although we could certainly use a hammer to drive a screw into a board, using a screwdriver would probably be more effective. Translation? Sometimes the Internet is the proper tool and sometimes it is not. Deciding which is which is outlined more in chapters 6 and 7.

Stages of Research

Research progresses sequentially through four basic stages or actions: (1) planning your work, (2) acquiring information, (3) writing your paper, and (4) revising your paper.

Planning Your Work

During this first stage, your primary goal is to learn about your assignment and develop a plan to complete it. Creating a time line for completion, developing your topic, and **brainstorming** about potential sources of information are among the many activities that take place in this stage. Some of the other activities at this stage include these:

- Identifying your specific information need(s)
- Brainstorming possible research strategies, resources, and terms
- Clearly articulating your topic, including drafting a **thesis**, or **purpose**, **statement** and related **research questions** you hope to answer through your research

Acquiring Information

The emphasis in this second stage is on implementing your plan to acquire the information you need to write your paper. As you acquire sources of information, you will need to evaluate them to make sure they are relevant and appropriate to your needs. As you learn more about your topic, it is extremely likely that you will revise your topic and refocus your research accordingly. Some of the activities at this stage are these:

- Finding source material
- Identifying source material that is relevant and appropriate to your information need
- Taking notes
- Revising your topic, research strategy, and completion time line

Writing Your Paper

Simply acquiring and evaluating the information are not sufficient. The third step of the research process is to synthesize the information you've collected and compile it into a logical, organized written paper. This doesn't mean just copying and pasting your notes into a paper. It means including information from sources but also your own insights into, interpretations of, and ideas about the topic. Some of the activities at this stage include the following:

- Organizing your source material in a logical pattern
- Synthesizing your source material into a readable narrative
- Addressing research "areas of need," such as the need for more sources
- Incorporating a variety of words and writing techniques into your narrative

Revising Your Paper

In this final stage, you try to polish your finished product for submission. Sometimes you will do this before your final paper is submitted. Other times, you will turn in your final paper, respond to comments and suggestions made by your instructor, and then resubmit. Either way, this phase typically involves editing, rewriting, and otherwise tweaking your paper until it's the best it can be. Some of the activities at this stage are these:

- Getting feedback on your writing about things such as flow, arrangement, and style
- Determining if assignment needs have been met
- Reviewing to ensure your research questions and purpose statement have been addressed
- Proofreading your writing for grammatical and typographical errors

Understanding the Research Process

Research is a process. If you simply sought sources and found them all the first time, that would be called *searching*. Because research is also a cycle, you are likely to search and search again to find what you want—or, literally, *re*-search. In fact, you may go through the various stages of the research process multiple times to greater or lesser degrees.

With that in mind, it is important to note that every researcher goes through similar stages and engages in similar activities throughout the research process. However, there is no perfect blueprint or single, right way to proceed through these stages and activities to ensure success. For example, some individuals begin their research by reading information on an area of interest and develop a topic accordingly. Others define a topic and revise it along the way as they encounter new information. Neither method for defining a topic is more right than the other.

The bottom line is that you need to develop your own personal research style that works for you. As you do so, be aware that what works for some researchers may not work for others. Likewise, know that all of the various research stages and activities you'll experience are interrelated. As a result, you can't ignore or neglect an aspect without detracting from the overall quality of your project. For example, you can't expect to write a good paper if you don't take good notes along the way. In the end, the degree to which you are both successful at each stage and effective at synthesizing each research activity plays a central role in determining your final grade.

It is important to note that the depth and breadth of every research project vary. However, the stages of the research process itself are well defined and common to all projects (see figure 1.2). Moreover, at each stage of the research process, beginning and expert researchers alike commonly experience similar emotions or reactions. The latter are outlined in figure 1.2. By familiarizing yourself with these stages and knowing ahead of time the feelings you are likely to experience, you will be better prepared to deal with and successfully navigate through them.

FIGURE 1.2

The (Re)Search Cycle

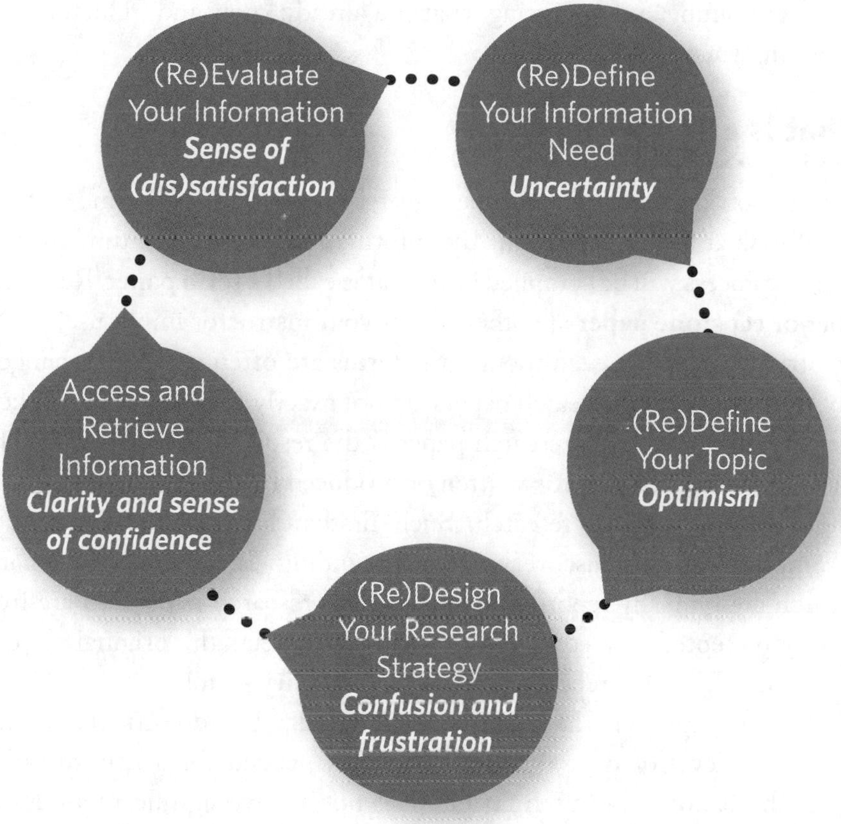

Here are two other important features to note about figure 1.2:

1. The research process is depicted as a cycle. Again, it can't be emphasized enough: research is not a straight-line, linear process. Effective, productive research often requires going through one or more stages multiple times before the project is completed. That is why it's called "*re*search" and not simply "search."

2. There is no clear starting point. Everyone enters the research cycle at different points and with different needs and expectations. Before you actually start a research project, for example,

you might already have considerable knowledge about your topic. As a result, rather than selecting a topic and beginning to look for background information, you may actually begin by examining and evaluating what you already know and (re)defining your topic accordingly.

What Is a Term Paper?

Having looked at research and the research process, it's now time to take a brief look at their application. The information you acquire through the research process will be compiled into what is called a **term paper**. Research paper or **capstone paper** are other names your instructor might use.

Strictly speaking, even though the terms are often used interchangeably, term papers and research papers are not exactly the same thing. A key distinction is that a true research paper is the result of **primary research**. That is, the research paper is written or produced by the individual(s) who conducted the original research. Such firsthand research often results in some sort of new discovery or understanding. The results of primary research are typically reported in an article or research paper and are frequently presented at a conference. Because it reflects the original or primary research, such a report is known as a **primary source**.

A term paper, on the other hand, is similar but doesn't necessarily involve the level or degree of sophistication needed for a true research paper. This is not to say a term paper does not involve significant amounts of research or time and effort. It does. However, rather than detailing the results of an experiment you conducted yourself, a term paper relies on information and source material produced by someone else. Such research is referred to as **secondary research**, and the sources used to produce the resultant report are called **secondary sources**.

To demonstrate the difference, suppose Researcher X is experimenting with a new technique to combat cancer.

Primary research: Because he would be the primary researcher, he is conducting primary research. In turn, his research paper would include such information as the experiment parameters, data collected and conclusions reached, potential side effects of the techniques, and similar facts discovered during the research process.

Secondary research: As a student, you decide to write a paper on experimental cancer treatments. The article Researcher X wrote shows up in one of your searches. You decide to use it. Because you neither wrote the article nor conducted the original research—you are merely reporting on the research of Researcher X—the article is a secondary source, and you are conducting secondary research.

A term paper . . .

- Involves secondary research
- Represents the final product of a semester- or term-long effort
- Is typically a written report
- Involves finding potential sources of information
- Reflects your values, perspectives, and personal experiences
- Requires analysis and evaluation of source material
- Synthesizes and connects source material in a meaningful way
- Uses and cites sources appropriately
- Varies in length (ten to fifteen pages is common)
- Demonstrates evidence of understanding the topic and the sources used
- Typically represents a significant portion of your final grade for a course

What a Term Paper Is Not

Many beginning researchers make the mistake of using a term paper to simply rehash key points about a topic or issue. However, a term paper is not simply a summary of key information. One of the main functions of a term paper is to demonstrate that you understand how the various pieces of information you've retrieved relate to one another. That is, a term paper should not simply summarize and regurgitate information. Rather, a term paper organizes information and places facts in context so that they have meaning and greater emphasis. In addition, many instructors will ask you to incorporate your own analyses, insights, and observations.

Most instructors will also expect you to address discrepancies among various sources and points of view you encounter. For example, one article might say eggs are an unhealthy food choice while another might state that they're good for us. Such seemingly contradictory sources shouldn't be ignored. In fact, addressing the contradictions is a good way to strengthen your overall paper. Some of the reasons behind these discrepancies are shown in figure 1.3.

FIGURE 1.3

Reasons for Discrepancies among Sources

Consideration	Example
Various contextual factors, such as culture, gender, and age, impact how a topic is researched and written about.	Someone who is twenty-five will understand and write about the concept of aging differently than will someone who has recently retired.
Information is outdated.	What we knew about cancer in 1954 was accurate at that time, but many advancements in cancer research have been made since then.
Definitions of terms and concepts differ.	Student success might be defined as earning a certain score on an exam or as achieving a certain graduation rate in a school district.
Interpretations of the data differ.	Saying 51 percent support something is no different from saying 49 percent do not.
Bias is present.	A Democrat is likely to have a different perspective about a candidate than is a Republican.

Elements of a Term Paper

Term papers typically consist of four common elements—abstract, introduction, body, conclusion—appearing in that order. The order of these elements and the content of any particular section, though, can vary by professor and by the type of term paper you write. Additional elements can include a bibliography or list of works cited.

Abstract

An **abstract** is essentially a summary. It provides an overview of key points, issues, findings, conclusions, and other information presented in your paper. Some professors will require an abstract and some will not.

Introduction

A term paper's **introduction** is usually rather brief, sometimes as short as a single paragraph. It is essentially a longer version of your purpose statement in that it introduces your topic, explains why you are writing the paper and how you are approaching the topic, and lists appropriate key points.

Body

The **body** is the main part of your paper. Incorporating your thesis statement and introduction, the body of your term paper is designed to prove your case. In the body, you cite and use experts' opinions to provide evidence in support of your purpose statement and to answer your research questions. If you're discussing a controversial topic, you'll typically provide supporting arguments as well as counterarguments critical of your thesis. If you're not using the work and opinions of others, your paper involves no research and is little more than an opinion piece or essay. If you're expected to inject your own ideas and observations, these would appear in the body as well.

Conclusion

Your **conclusion** shouldn't introduce any new material that you haven't already covered. Instead, it should reflect on key points you've made, synthesizing and otherwise pulling together all the information you've presented in the body of your work. In that context, your conclusion should refer to your research questions and overall purpose statement.

Works Cited/References/Bibliography

When you use someone else's ideas in your paper, you must credit her or him. A **works cited** page lists the sources of information you used to write your paper. This is sometimes referred to as a **bibliography** or **reference page**. There are many **citation style manuals** (also called **style guides** and **style manuals**) and other forms of assistance available to help you with this part of your paper. Some instructors of introductory courses are more concerned about consistency of **citations** than they are about mastery of a given **citation style**. Either way, you should check with your instructor, who can direct you to appropriate resources and provide insight into how perfect your citations need to be for your paper.

Other

Some instructors may ask you to include other, nonstandard elements as part of your term paper. These may be such things as a title page, a list of figures or graphics used, and an **appendix**. In addition, before submitting your **final draft**, you might be asked to submit an outline, your notes, or **rough drafts** of your progress at certain stages. Being asked to submit a list of search terms and strategies is also not uncommon. However, though important to the overall research process, these items typically are not included as part of a standard term paper but are submitted as auxiliary assignments supporting your final paper.

Getting It Done

What does it take to successfully complete a term paper? Being curious about your topic is certainly key. You also have to be able to lengthen your attention span. Having a working knowledge of how to access and use information search tools and being comfortable with writing, editing, and rewriting are also central. Other useful skills and traits include patience, problem- and puzzle-solving ability, a working familiarity with computers, time management, stress management, humility, perseverance, reading comprehension, and organization.

Two Final Thoughts

Two of the most common errors student researchers make are trying to do too much and doing too little. Both approaches are equally problematic and will significantly diminish the quality of your final paper. Knowing when to ask for advice from your instructor is critical in addressing both of these concerns.

Doing Too Much

Overachievers and those extremely motivated by their topic often fall into the trap of trying to exhaust their topic. In an attempt to pursue every possible angle on their topic, some individuals try to find and include *every* piece of information they can. Sometimes individuals are simply not focused and try to weave together a lot of marginally related pieces of information. Others continue to edit well past the point of diminishing returns.

☑ TIPS

- Review your purpose statement and focus your work accordingly.
- (Re)Focus your purpose statement and research questions.
- Talk with your instructor to determine when enough is enough.

Doing Too Little

At the other end of the spectrum are those individuals who try to do as little as possible. For example, some individuals wait until the last minute, having to pull an **all-nighter** to get their paper done. Among other things, this approach results in poor quality source material and hurried writing, producing a paper that feels thrown together. Others use the first sources of information they find regardless of whether those sources are relevant or appropriate. Some even try to bypass assignment requirements by changing their fonts, margins, and more to make a short paper seem longer. Simply put, it's usually pretty easy to detect who has put forth effort and who has not. For those who don't, the overall quality of the final product is diminished significantly and almost always guarantees a lower grade. In the long run, you'll be far more successful (and happy) if you do some planning early and complete your research project in stages.

☑ TIPS

- Pace yourself by doing your work in a focused way over an extended period rather than in short, unfocused, compressed bursts.
- Keep in mind that it generally takes less time and effort to do something right the first time than it does to go back later and correct your mistakes.

❷ REFLECTIONS

- What is the longest paper you've ever written?
- Have you ever done research before? What was easy for you? With what aspects did you struggle?
- If you've never done research before, what is your biggest concern or fear?
- In talking with your classmates, what sorts of things do you hear about research or the research process?
- Is it easy or difficult for you to ask for and act on feedback?

CHAPTER 2

Preparing for Research

. . . .

Beginning researchers often enter the research process with little or no understanding of what to do or expect. As a result, they are often afraid of doing research and quickly become frustrated and overwhelmed. For example, many times the problem isn't finding articles or writing the paper as much as it is managing time and taking notes. First-time researchers are frequently unaware of, or overlook the significance of, these auxiliary considerations. However, being aware of them before you begin will go a long way toward reducing or even eliminating many of the challenges you'll encounter throughout your research.

"The Dirty Dozen"
. . . .

If you are unfamiliar or uncomfortable with research, you may not know exactly what skills and abilities you need to do research, let alone what your strengths and weaknesses—and, yes, your fears—might be. Although it probably goes without saying, you should work to identify and address your fears and weaknesses. Doing so will help you anticipate where you are likely to face hurdles along the way.

In turn, an honest assessment will help you to budget your time and effort more effectively by enabling you to capitalize on your strengths and minimize the impact of your weaknesses as you move through the research cycle. For example, if you struggle with writing, you may want to find a tutor, contact your school's writing center, or find someone with good writing and editing skills who is willing to help you. Obviously such connections take time to establish. So, waiting till you actually start writing may not be your best plan of action.

Although you need many and varied skills to complete a term paper, the following twelve are the most essential. You must be able to . . .

1. Evaluate source material for **relevancy** and **accuracy**
2. Analyze the arguments of others
3. Formulate and express your own arguments
4. Distinguish between fact and opinion
5. Synthesize various pieces of information
6. Work independently
7. Read for comprehension
8. Focus your attention for extended periods
9. Meet a **deadline**
10. Access and retrieve information efficiently and effectively
11. Organize and coordinate a variety of tasks and activities
12. Write and edit well and cite source material properly

Ask for Help!

Reread the section heading: *Ask for Help!* Now, read it again to be sure you remember it. To a large extent, your term paper's success depends on your understanding and application of this simple three-word phrase.

Ask for Help!

In short, you need to ask for help when you're experiencing difficulty. Go into the research process knowing that *every* veteran and rookie researcher alike struggles at some point in the research process. But also recognize that, as with most things, the more you do something, the easier it becomes.

Ask for Help!

Research is no different in this respect. Yes, the skill set in the preceding section is intimidating and looks daunting. You may not know which search tools to use or how to access them. You may never have read a scholarly article before. There are any number of things that you simply may not have ever done before or that you are not as good at doing as you could be.

Rest assured, you are not expected to be an expert researcher at this stage. Few people are good at all twelve skills, and certainly not those who are doing a term paper for the first time or who have not done so recently.

Ask for Help!

That said, it is important to keep in mind that you shouldn't struggle unnecessarily. Don't spend five weeks trying to decide on a topic or three hours trying to locate the perfect article. Spend a reasonable amount of time trying to solve the problem yourself. Some challenges are fairly straightforward and merely require time and effort to resolve. However, when you truly are stuck, speak with someone who is able to help you. Two of the best in this regard are your instructor and a **librarian**. Another benefit of planning is to be able to talk with someone early, before the problem explodes on you, rather than waiting till the last minute when it may not be possible to effectively remedy the concern. Talking to an expert can also be a great stress reliever and a way to gain some confidence about where you are in the process.

Instructor

Your instructor should always be your first line of defense. At the very least, because he created the assignment, he can tell you what's expected, where you need to focus, and more. He has also gone through the research process before—on his own and while assisting his students.

Librarian

Although this might be the first time you've done research, a librarian assists students with research all day long. Therefore, she is very familiar with research and possible sources of information. In fact, she is often familiar with your research assignment because she has worked with your instructor to develop it. It's even more likely that she has helped one or more of your classmates trying to complete it.

☑ **TIPS** ────────────────────────────────

- Recognize that you're not alone—others have succeeded before and others are going through this now.

- Set aside additional time to address your problem areas (e.g., writing, reading comprehension, **proofreading**).
- Identify the departments (e.g., writing centers, research labs), groups, and individuals (e.g., tutors) who offer the kind of help you need and visit with them as needed.
- Ask for help!

Stay Focused

Maintaining focus throughout the life of a term paper is extremely challenging for many individuals, particularly first-time researchers. For one thing, college presents a lot of distractions. Socializing, going to an athletic event, and participating in a host of other activities can easily draw your attention away from your academic work. In addition, we've grown accustomed to receiving and processing information in short bursts, such as through e-mail and text messages. Such sources require little focus and can generally be addressed in a few minutes or even seconds.

Research is different in that it requires you to maintain focus, often for an extended period. This alone makes it easy to lose focus sometimes. Beyond that though, you need to read, digest, synthesize, and organize *a lot* of information over the course of the semester. Maintaining focus is made even more difficult by the fact that reading academic material is different and typically more time-consuming than leisure reading. The concepts and vocabulary can be challenging, and the writing can be rather dry. These and other factors make it easy to lose your focus and move on to something else.

✔ TIPS

- Practice regularly engaging in extended academic and intellectual activities. For example, try reading for thirty minutes or more without distractions, breaks, or additional stimulation.
- Determine whether you work best in a quiet, distraction-free environment or whether you work better with a little distraction such as background music.
- Find a location that best suits the way you study and complete academic work.

- Strive to work around or avoid known distractions such as your roommate's family visiting for the day or homecoming weekend.
- Divide whatever you're working on into smaller, more manageable parts.

Identify and Address Access Issues Early

Many beginning researchers overlook access. You can't assume that the library will be open when you want to use it or that you can print an unlimited number of pages or even that the resource you used last semester is still available. For electronic resources, you might also need to establish some form of user account or download software in order to gain access. Although such access issues are not insurmountable, the stress they can create can generally be minimized or avoided altogether with a little planning and foresight.

☑ TIPS

- Determine when your library is open.
- Identify the log-in or **authentication** procedure for accessing library resources from off-site.
- If you don't already have them, determine what you need to do to gain remote access privileges, and get them.
- Be sure you have a removable storage device such as a flash drive or access to cloud-based or other networked storage locations with sufficient memory to store your work.
- Because many institutions don't provide unlimited printing, you need to learn how and how much you can print.
- Decide how much you're willing to spend if there is a cost to acquire a book or article or other source of information.

Acknowledge and Manage Your Stress

Research can be extremely stressful. The fact that a term paper can occupy your attention for an entire term can result in that stress lasting a long time. This does not mean you should plan to work on your term paper 24/7. That's neither healthy nor realistic. Still, you need to know what sorts of things cause you stress, how those stressors make you feel and behave, and, most importantly, how to reduce or eliminate their impact on you and your work. Everyone stresses over different things. Similarly, everyone deals with stress differently. As a result, you need to find the way that works for you and not be afraid to use it when you need it.

☑ TIPS

- Take time each day to relax.
- Make a point to regularly do something you enjoy.
- Break the project down into smaller, more manageable parts.
- Engage in healthy activities, eat healthy food, and get plenty of rest.

Timing Is Everything

From start to finish, arguably one of the most challenging and stressful aspects of research is time management. As will be said again and again … researching and writing a term paper are time-consuming activities requiring considerable focus, effort, and organization to be successful. Because the **due date** for term papers is typically at the end of the semester, it's easy to get the false impression that there's lots of time and no need to begin working till much later in the term. Unfortunately, the end of the semester comes all too quickly. Students who understand their relationship to time will generally be better managers of their time and, in turn, produce better papers, experience far less stress, and have fewer problems along the way than those who do not.

Three things to understand about your relationship with time are outlined in the following sections. By reflecting on each and placing it into a meaningful context, you will be better equipped to manage your time and effort more effectively.

Time of Day

When is the best time of day for you to do academic work? If you're a morning person, it's probably best to budget some time for working on your research project in the morning—the time you are most alert and likely to do good work. Similarly, if you need quiet to study and you know that the marching band practices outside your window at 3:00 p.m., it's probably a good idea to do your work before then or wait until the band has gone.

Procrastination

Being a procrastinator isn't bad or wrong. But, in the context of conducting research, it can be extremely problematic. As noted earlier, students often underestimate the amount of time it will take to complete a term paper. Because of the amount of effort involved and the amount of coordination necessary to complete a term paper, putting things off and delaying their completion is not advisable. Budgeting your time and doing a little bit of work each day will generally be less stressful and frustrating than waiting till the last minute and trying to do everything at once.

Delays

Researchers often encounter problems that can delay the research process and completion of the term paper. Delays are as common for beginning researchers as they are for those with more experience. Some delays can be reduced or even avoided; others will be completely out of your control. Some will be long; others will be brief. The nature and variety of possible delays vary from individual to individual and comprise a broad spectrum of concerns from procrastination to writer's block to computer crashes and more. Rest assured, though, delays are a part of the research process and should be expected.

The following are three of the more common challenges likely to cause delays or otherwise slow your research progress.

1. *Inexperience*: Never having done research before or not having done so recently can cause significant delays. For beginners, lack of familiarity with the research process is a common problem. They often have difficulty knowing where to begin or how to overcome challenges they face along the way. The same is true, albeit in a somewhat different way, for students who have been out of school for a while or who don't conduct research often. Because resources change all the time, for example, the strategies that worked last time may or may not

work this time. In both cases, extra time must be spent overcoming this delay.

2. *Obligations*: Research doesn't have a monopoly on this challenge. Determining the right amount of time and effort to devote to your personal, family, academic, professional, and other commitments can be challenging even without having to do a term paper. Worse, many of these commitments erupt without notice. Being called to pick up your sick child from school during the time you'd budgeted to conduct research can't be helped. Setting priorities and balancing commitments are acts each of us does every day. Needing to complete a term paper is just one more obligation to add to the list.

3. *Being overwhelmed*: This is a corollary to all of the preceding. Simply having to do too much can cause one to feel overwhelmed. Even if there are not a lot of tasks, life itself can become overwhelming. To use a personal example, from 2004 to 2008, I was pursuing my doctorate and had to drive three hours just to get to class. In addition to handling a full course load, I was working on my dissertation and continuing to work full time. On top of that, during this same four-year period, I got married, my wife and I moved, and we had a baby. Needless to say, there were many times I felt overwhelmed. Unfortunately, there is no cure-all that works for everyone. Just recognize that you're likely to feel overwhelmed at some point and will need to know how to handle the upheaval and stress that such feelings can generate.

Create a Research Time Line

Creating a **research time line** (and sticking to it!) is one of the best ways to overcome many time-related challenges and reduce your stress. Think of a time line as a pie. If you try to eat the whole thing at once, it's likely to be messy and unpleasant. By slicing the pie into pieces, though, it becomes much more manageable. Research is no different. Having a time line breaks the project into several smaller, more manageable stages.

Figure 2.1 is a very simplistic time line for completing a term paper. The first column provides an itemized list of activities to be completed, the second column indicates the specific date you plan to complete the activity, and the third shows the amount of time to be devoted to each task. If the dates in column two are not the same as the actual due date for a particular activity, you should include such deadlines in your time line. This will help you visualize exactly when a particular activity needs to be completed, not just the date by which you plan to complete it.

FIGURE 2.1

Sample Time Line for Term Paper

Activity	Date	Time Needed
Assignment received	September 1	September 1
Preliminary topic identified	September 19	2–2½ weeks
Preliminary research conducted	October 3	2 weeks
Tom's wedding	October 5	October 5–7
Topic revised/finalized	October 10	1 week
Preliminary research completed	October 17	1 week
Work on rough draft	October 31	2 weeks
Rough draft due	November 3	November 3
Final research completed	November 7	4 days
Work on final draft	November 18	1–1½ weeks
Thanksgiving break	November 19–23	5 days
Proofread and complete final draft	December 11	2–2½ weeks
Assignment due	December 12	December 12

 TIPS

- When budgeting time for a given activity, always include a little extra to accommodate unforeseen problems and circumstances that might arise, such as power outages or a family emergency.

- Budget additional time to address known areas of weakness. Writing, for example, may require working with a tutor or your campus's writing center, either of which will take additional time.
- Include known obligations, such as your best friend Tom's wedding, as well as open time for things like holiday breaks that will have a significant impact on the time you can devote to your project.

Adopt New Reading Strategies

On a number of levels, how you read when conducting research is very different from how you read when reading for pleasure. With leisure books, for example, you probably don't spend a lot of time (if any) doing things like taking notes or figuring out how what you read fits in with other things you have read or learned. Your focus is primarily on enjoying the story or topic of the book. Conversely, when reading for research purposes, activities such as comprehending, evaluating, and synthesizing the material are critical. To accomplish these goals, you need to engage in a number of reading strategies to become a successful "research reader" and to make the best use of your time and effort.

Skimming

As the name suggests, **skimming** involves going over materials at a basic, surface level and is an excellent tool for determining the relevance of a given source. The main objective is not to know and understand every point being made but, rather, to determine whether the piece is relevant and worth reading in more detail later. As you skim, you should also be alert for areas or sections of content that warrant greater attention. These will be the areas for you to focus on more heavily when you reread the item in more depth later.

In addition to the qualitative differences, many students are intimidated by the quantity of reading a term paper requires. Is this true? Yes, to an extent. Conducting research for a term paper does require a lot of reading. But does this mean that you need to read every single word of the eight books, fifteen articles, and seven websites on your list of possible sources? No.

- For articles, scan the title, read the abstract, read the first and last paragraph; for scholarly articles, also scan the results or conclusions section.
- For books, scan the title, table of contents, index, introduction, and first chapter.
- Place your sources in four piles: use, possibly use, explore further, don't use.
- As you skim, jot down names, words, phrases, and other specific information that you can use to refine your search strategy and research direction.
- Scan the reference list for possible additional source material.
- Always focus on why you are reading and what you are hoping to find.

Grasping the Main Ideas

Grasping the main idea or ideas behind what you're reading is obviously very critical to the research process. The main idea is the most significant aspect, important point, or focus of a paragraph. Although it is typically found in the first sentence of a paragraph, this is not always the case. Regardless of where it is found, the main idea announces or summarizes the central theme of what you're reading.

To determine the main idea, you need to ask yourself what is being said. The main idea will reflect the author's view on the person, thought, concept, or topic being discussed. The rest of the information contained in a paragraph is supporting information, providing more details about the topic. Although they are certainly important, details will lack meaning without context and an understanding of the main idea being presented.

TIPS

- Read the first sentence of each paragraph for main points to be presented.
- Review the abstract or summary, findings, conclusion, and discussion sections.
- After you've read a passage or section, try to summarize what you've read in a single sentence.

- Look for words, phrases, and ideas that are repeated because they are likely to reflect on or revolve around the main idea.
- Underline the sentence that provides the main idea of a paragraph.
- In addition to specific content, take notes on concepts, how the concepts are used or defined, and how the author arrives at conclusions.

Reading Critically

When you read something critically, you are not just reading. You are evaluating what you read for both relevance and accuracy (see chapter 10). **Critical reading** involves comparing and contrasting other items you have read or experienced. It involves examining the historical, cultural, and other contexts of the information to better understand it. For example, one source might say a certain factor causes cancer while another says that such claims are unfounded. Examining the context, you might learn the former source was written in 1945. A lot of new information about carcinogens has been produced in the decades since. This doesn't mean that the first claim is wrong and the second is right. It simply demonstrates the need to understand the context in which the information is presented.

✓ TIPS

- Use main ideas restated in your own words to create an outline.
- Reflect on ideas and concepts that challenge your own values and beliefs.
- Make connections between your readings by looking for similarities as well as differences.
- Develop a working understanding of unknown terms, concepts, and ideas.

Reading for Comprehension

Reading is a productive activity only to the extent that you understand what you have read. For example, the article you are reading might be the best article on your topic, but if you do not understand it or how you can incorporate it into your paper, your reading of it will not be a very productive use of your time.

Once you begin reading for comprehension (versus skimming for main ideas), you need to be able to make sense of what you read. At a minimum, this means understanding what has been written. But you also need to be able to synthesize key points and ideas and connect them with others you have come across in your research. At the same time, you need to be able to critically evaluate information and eliminate any that is irrelevant or inaccurate. You also need to be able to focus on and remember what you have read.

☑ **TIPS** ────────────────────────────────

- Review what you do and do not understand and restate the difficult parts in your own words.
- Generate questions as a way to understand what you have read.
- Combine information from different parts of the text or from other sources you have already read.
- Summarize what you have read as a means of identifying main ideas and connecting them with one another.

Develop a Method for Taking Notes

Remember that research is a process involving many interrelated steps and activities. Moreover, it is not a series of discrete steps that necessarily occur sequentially. As a result, you will need to develop an organizational style and technique that work for you to ensure that events flow relatively smoothly throughout the process. Lacking such, matters can get confusing very quickly and result in added stress and other problems.

A key part of your success in this regard is to develop an effective and efficient means of taking notes. How you do so is entirely up to you. All kinds of techniques and strategies exist. Because it is such a critical aspect of the research process, though, you need to find a note-taking method that works for you. Whatever method you adopt should provide a meaningful and navigable way to record the main ideas and key concepts of the information you've acquired. It should also enable you to quickly identify which notes came from which source.

Grab a Pen, Not a Highlighter!

When you take notes, identifying key concepts and terms in the text is obviously very important. Highlighting text with a colored marker as you read is a good way to do so. It enables you to draw attention to relevant passages for further reading. Highlighting also makes it easy to identify terms and concepts you can use to generate additional search strategies.

However, simply highlighting text alone is not enough. You need to be sure you understand what you have read. Writing notes (versus merely highlighting text) forces you to comprehend what you have read well enough to put it into your own words. You are also far more likely to remember notes you have written than text you have simply highlighted. Furthermore, taking notes has the advantage of enabling you to interject your own thoughts and observations. Conversely, when rereading text, if you focus *only* on the highlighted sections, you will likely miss the context and, in turn, overlook or not understand key points being made by the author.

Types of Notes

In general, you will be taking three types of notes (outlined in this section). Because each type serves a different purpose, it is important to keep track of distinctions between them.

1. *Content*: This type of note focuses on the main ideas, concepts, and other information you uncover as you read. In addition to making specific content notes, maintaining a running list of details like key terms, names, and dates will assist you in formulating additional research strategies and directions.

2. *Personal*: These notes revolve around personal thoughts and insights that occur to you as you read. They may range from opinions to additional content areas to explore to your feelings and observations as you read. They are subjective. You may see fit to incorporate them into your paper directly or use them as potential avenues for additional research.

3. *Citation information*: One critical element often overlooked by beginning researchers is citation information. Citations will be discussed in greater detail in chapter 11. For now, suffice it to say that a citation provides information about the source of your information. Not only does it give credit to the person who originally generated the information, a citation also provides a trail back to the original source.

On a practical level, as part of your final paper, you will be expected to supply a complete list of sources you have used. As you read, you will need to record citation information for the sources you are thinking of using. In turn, you will need to have an organized method for recording this information. The resultant list will enable you to produce your list of sources more quickly and efficiently. Unfortunately, many beginning researchers forget or are not aware that they need this information as they begin taking notes. They then have to spend considerable time and effort re-researching to find their original source material in order to produce a citation.

Note-Taking Strategies

There are a number of note-taking strategies, each with its own advantages and disadvantages. Whatever method you select, it should be one that you are comfortable with and that makes it easy to complete your final paper. Two common note-taking strategies follow.

Columns

Make two columns on a sheet of paper. Use the first column to jot down main ideas and the other to record specific details or information. Some recommend a third column wherein you include notes about new thoughts and ideas that occur to you while reading and similar information about how the material might lead to new sources or otherwise be incorporated into your paper. Although this method provides a context for your notes, it can be a challenge sifting through them once you start to write.

Index Cards

For this note-taking method, you use index cards. The idea is to place only one note or concept on a single card. When it is time to write your paper, you simply place the cards in the order that makes the most sense. The manageability of this method is one of its strengths.

However, this method can be somewhat cumbersome because of the number of cards you may have by the time you complete your research. Some also advocate placing the author's thoughts on one side of the card and yours on the other. This technique, though, can obviously make it challenging to place the cards in order as described earlier. What if you choose not to include your opinion (on side two) till later? Do you make an additional card (cumbersome), or do you somehow hope to remember the thought later on?

As an alternative, some suggest placing citation information on the back of the card. The greatest advantage of this method is that it ensures you know which thoughts and ideas came from which source. This technique will make generating citations and the creation of your references page much easier. But if you use this method, you'll likely want to develop some way of abbreviating the process so that you don't have to write the complete citation every time. Whatever method you use, it is imperative that *every* card is labeled in some way so that, if it becomes separated, you know which card is associated with which source of information.

Finally, if you use the card method for note-taking, be sure to (a) flip every card over and back to ensure you haven't overlooked any important information and (b) make certain you know which side represents your thoughts and which represents the source's.

Citation-Specific Notes

Whatever method you employ to take notes, you also need to develop some means of recording information about the source from which your notes were generated. Two of these are summarized in this section. Again, the information you need to record will be discussed in greater detail in chapter 11. For now, know that to cite a source, you will need such details as the author's name, the title of the source, page numbers, and similar identifying information to provide a path back to the original.

Cover Card or Page

One strategy is to include the citation information on the first card or page of notes for a given source. Then, when you need to compile your list of sources, you can simply look at the first card or page of notes to determine their origin. A significant drawback to this approach is that the first page or card might become detached. Still, if you are careful, this technique is quick and easy and very straightforward.

Cross-Reference

Another common technique is to keep a running list of sources and cross-reference them. That is, rather than use a single page as just noted, you code each note or page of notes. At the same time, you keep a running list of all the sources you examine. When it is time to produce your list of sources, you look at the codes for the notes you used and refer to your composite list for the matching source information. This involves more effort than the preceding technique, but it ensures you don't lose citation information.

For example, your list might look something like the following. If you use a note with the code "Jones1," you can look at this list and determine that the note came from *The Secret Life of Dogs*.

Jones1   The Secret Life of Dogs. Albert Jones. Pet Press, New York, 2002.

Smith2   Dog Days Are Over. Rachel Smith. The Journal of Pet Therapy, Volume 3, Issue 7, pages 13–25.

☑ TIPS

- Write legibly—it may be several days or weeks before you try to read your notes, and you need to be able to read what you wrote.
- Don't write everything down unless it's an *exact* quote, and if it is, include it in quotation marks ("like this") to distinguish quotes from notes.
- Include page numbers for every direct quotation.
- Don't take notes on everything—focus on such elements as key concepts and how they're used or defined, conclusions, dates, and names.
- Label each note, outlining the focus of the note.
- Minimize the number of index cards by including your own thoughts and ideas on the back.
- Even though the citation feature of many electronic resources provides you with the necessary content for a citation, it is your responsibility to ensure that the content is accurate and that the citation you provide is properly formatted.

Copy or Print All Sources

Looking ahead to when you begin writing your paper, you may find at some point that you need to reread one of your sources to better understand a particular concept, or you may want to double-check whether you're quoting a source accurately. Having a copy on hand will enable you to do this much more efficiently than if you have to track down the item again. Many instructors will ask you to provide copies of sources you have used, particularly early in the process. Among other things, this requirement helps them to guide you in the right direction.

Articles: Make a digital or printed copy of the article and, either as part of that copy or separately, make a copy of relevant citation information.

Books: Make copies of the appropriate pages, sections, or chapters as well as the pages containing citation information, such as the title page. Consider copying the table of contents to help you quickly locate additional material later.

Websites: Because websites disappear all the time, it's especially important to make copies while you're accessing sites. In addition to relevant content, be sure your copy includes the URL for the site and the date you accessed it.

Citations: Many resources enable you to copy and paste citation information. However, although they often provide all the necessary citation information, be warned that these citations are often formatted incorrectly. Ultimately, it is your responsibility to ensure that the information is accurate and properly formatted.

Build Computer Fluency

Research is increasingly dependent on technology. More and more information is being produced and stored electronically every day. Some of the many skills and strategies you need to successfully navigate information technologies are discussed in chapter 8. In addition, though, you need a variety of basic computing skills. A working knowledge of word processing, for example, is essential. Two skills many students overlook in preparing for research are saving their work and, even more so, making backup copies.

Saving Files

Many times, your instructor will ask you to turn in each successive draft you write. Even if you are not asked to do so, you are still likely to generate a number of drafts and revisions before producing your final paper. As part of the research process, you are also likely to collect and produce all sorts of working files and documents, such as your notes and articles and other information you plan to read or use. To save yourself time and avoid confusion later, it is a good idea early in the process to develop some standard way to name your files. For example, it is not clear if "Draft" refers to your first draft, final draft, or some draft in between.

☑ TIPS

- Filenames should be brief yet descriptive.
- Add numbers to reduce confusion between older and more recent versions and to keep files in order (versus alphabetical order). *Note*: Adding a zero at the start will ensure 1 comes before 10.

     Example:
     01 Gray wolves
     02 Domestic dogs
     03 Canines

- Because many institutions employ software that periodically erases personal files stored on workstation hard drives every week (or even every day), it is a good idea to save your work to a network or a removable drive.
- For articles, try syncing your filenames with your style of note-taking. In the example discussed earlier, use "Jones1" to associate file notes from the source material you identified as having come from "Jones1."
- Including a date in the filename each time you save your document helps ensure you're working on the most current version (e.g., "Literature review 012315.docx").
- Create (sub)folders to store different pieces of your project (e.g., articles, drafts, images) to help you stay organized throughout the research process.

Making Backup Copies

Many students do not make backup copies of their work. They offer many reasons, ranging from claiming it is unnecessary to maintaining it takes too much time. Admittedly, the original file is sufficient for the overwhelming majority of students. Unfortunately, it only takes the loss of a file one time to convince them that backup copies are worthwhile. Although the following story is a worst-case scenario, it makes a simple point: if it's important enough to save once, it's probably important enough to save twice.

I will never forget my experience with a master's degree student several years ago. She came to the library on a Thursday to print a copy of her thesis with the intent of then delivering it to her advisor so that she could graduate that Saturday. When she approached me, she was crying: her file would not open, and she had no backup copy. I eventually managed to recover about seventy-five pages. Of what was legible (only about half), the formatting was completely off. Worse, more than twenty other pages simply weren't there. Worst of all? None of the data she'd collected could be recovered. For all intents and purposes, three years of her life had been erased.

✔ TIPS

- If possible, store backup copies in a location different from that of your original files.
- Should your storage device get stolen, your backup copy can help prove the file submitted by someone else is actually yours.
- Back up your files regularly and often—it only takes a few additional seconds.
- When saving a draft or making a backup copy, use Save As (rather than Save) to avoid overwriting your original file.

❓ REFLECTIONS

- Rate your ability with each of the following on a scale from 1 (high) to 5 (low). For each item that you rate 3 or more, identify the person or office at your school to contact for help.
  - ‣ Writing
  - ‣ Comprehending what I read

- Locating books and articles
- Editing
- Citing my sources
- Managing my time
- Spelling
- Typing
- Working independently
- Summarizing
- Organizing
- Staying focused
- Taking effective notes
- Managing stress
- Making connections between ideas

- What is your instructor's name? Building and office number? Telephone number? E-mail address? Preferred method of contact? Office hours?

- To help see where your time goes and to help you more effectively budget the time you have left, draft a weekly and monthly calendar. Include your class schedule as well as events such as meals, known obligations (e.g., work, doctor's appointment), and activities in which you are involved (e.g., athletic teams). Once that's done, incorporate your research time line outlined earlier in this chapter. Budget time (one to two hours) that you will regularly commit to working on your term paper.

- Sync your calendar with your phone, e-mail, and so on so you have constant access to it as both a reminder and a motivator.

- When you read the following, how is your reading different? How is it the same?

  - Poem
  - Magazine
  - Nonfiction book
  - First-year biology textbook
  - Website
  - Newspaper
  - Novel (fiction)
  - Advertisement

- When reading, what do you do when you read a term you don't know or come across a concept you don't understand?

- Research is increasingly dependent on technology. The following are some of the basic computer skills you need to facilitate your research. If you are unfamiliar with or unclear about how to use or perform any of the following, find someone who can assist you.

  - ▸ Save versus Save As commands
  - ▸ Redo versus Undo commands
  - ▸ Print versus Print Preview commands
  - ▸ Making a backup copy of a file
  - ▸ Locating files you have saved
  - ▸ Cutting, copying, and pasting text and images
  - ▸ Highlighting a selection of text
  - ▸ Formatting images
  - ▸ Wrapping text (around images)
  - ▸ Printing a selection of pages (rather than a whole document)

CHAPTER 3

Understanding Libraries and Librarians

. . . .

With the Internet, information has become available virtually any-time, anywhere. As a result, people can easily access information on their own. Still, it is a rare researcher who doesn't need help with some aspect of research. Whether it's picking a topic or sifting through the sheer volume of information, libraries and librarians provide assistance with these and virtually every other aspect of the research process.

What Is a Library?

When people think of libraries, all sorts of images come to mind. Some of these images are accurate, many are not or are seriously outdated, and most fall somewhere in between. So what exactly *is* a library? Big or small, specialized or general, academic or public—at its core, a library is essentially any collection of recorded information.

- The word *library* is derived from the Latin word *liber* meaning "book."
- Libraries have existed for thousands of years.
- The first libraries were used primarily to store business, historical, religious, and other records of a person, town, country, or civilization.
- Because early books had to be handwritten, copies were very scarce and very valuable; they were generally inaccessible to all but the wealthy.

- By the late Middle Ages, with the invention of paper and the printing press, books began to be more affordable and more commonplace; the modern library began to emerge.
- As the quantity and variety of books grew, new ways of storing and organizing them had to be developed. Shelving books by subject continues to be the most common.
- The focus of today's library is increasingly on access to information rather than on ownership of it.

Reasons Students Do *Not* Go to the Library

Many first-time researchers overlook the library as a starting point when beginning the research process. Some students still think of libraries as little more than book warehouses and don't realize the wealth of other information sources that libraries provide. Lingering stereotypes of taciturn, unapproachable, "shushing" librarians still abound, intimidating would-be library users. Other reasons that some students question or otherwise overlook the value of using the library to conduct research include the following:

- "I've never had to use a library before."
- "I can get everything I need off the Internet."
- "I won't ask librarians for help because I don't really know what they do or what type of assistance they can provide."
- "I don't even know where to begin."

Reasons Students *Should* Go to the Library

Most of the myths just outlined contain a certain degree of truth. That said, today's modern library is more than just a huge collection of books and a staff intent on making sure no one speaks above a whisper. Libraries are active, vibrant places reflecting the changing information needs and the collaborative viewpoint of today's learner. Vast collections of printed books and journals, for example, are being replaced with electronic access to the same material, and "shushing" librarians are being replaced with librarians who provide open, common areas where groups are encouraged to work together and share ideas—verbally and via technology. Here are a few of the many reasons that going to the library and speaking with a librarian should be high on your research agenda:

- Libraries provide access to information and resources not available elsewhere, particularly to old, rare, or out-of-print resources but also to newer content.
- Libraries offer a breadth and depth of services, including **circulation**, **reference**, and interlibrary loan, as well as resources beyond simply books and magazines, such as movies, music, artwork, and even snack bars.
- If your library doesn't provide direct access to the resource you want—especially an article or a book—a librarian can typically get it from another library for you.
- Libraries provide study space, equipment, technology, and other resources and services to assist you in your research and academic pursuits. Examples of these auxiliary services include **writing centers** and tutoring.
- Librarians are trained in the use of information resources and have vast experience with the research process and finding information.

It is important to note at this point that perhaps the most important reason for going to the library is the librarians. One of a librarian's primary jobs is to help you find and use relevant information. In fact, for some librarians, this is their main, and sometimes only, duty. They can help you understand and navigate through your assignment. A librarian can direct you to the best resources, suggest search strategies, and do a whole lot more. When you encounter a challenge in the research process—and you will—a librarian will typically be able to help you or at least offer some suggestions for working through it.

Library Types

There are many types of libraries. All libraries can loosely be grouped into one of four broad categories: academic, public, school, and special. The library at your college or university is an academic library. You may need to use the resources and services of multiple libraries or library types to complete your research.

Academic

Because it supports the curriculum, research, teaching, and information needs of a college or university, an **academic library** focuses primarily on academic, scholarly sorts of books, journals, and other resources. Items such as best sellers and popular music may be part of the collection but only minimally unless the school offers courses that involve those elements. Larger universities may have more than one library to serve specific needs, such as a medical library for a medical school. Many academic libraries are open long after other departments and buildings on campus have closed, providing an ideal venue for studying and for completing academic work.

Public

A **public library** serves the community in which it is located. The emphasis is on leisure reading and other items of interest to the general population. Best sellers and self-help books are good examples. Many public libraries have specialized departments that focus on a specific population (e.g., children, teens) or interest (e.g., genealogy).

School

A **school library** is associated with K–12 schools or school districts. School libraries are learner-centered and focus on ensuring that all students have access to information. They typically contain books, **periodicals**, and various media for both educational and entertainment purposes.

Special

A **special library** encompasses everything else. Special libraries gear their resources and services to a specific topic or population. For example, a business library focuses on books and other items pertaining specifically to business and business-related topics. Similarly, a library for the blind provides items such as books in braille and devices for converting text to speech to better serve those with visual difficulties. Special libraries can have large collections or small ones. They may be open to the public or may restrict access to individuals associated with their parent business, school, or organization. Examples of where you might find a special library include hospitals, medical schools, law schools, seminaries, museums, government agencies, and many large corporations and businesses.

Anatomy of an Academic Library

Academic libraries can be intimidating. They often occupy one of the largest buildings on campus, and large campuses often have more than one library. In addition, they contain a number of departments, operations, and services that can further overwhelm a first-time researcher. However, most academic libraries have at least four areas in common and with which you'll likely be working at some point during your research journey.

Circulation

Usually located at or near the entrance to a library, the **circulation desk** is where you go to check out, return, and renew books and other items, pay fines, get general information, and more. It is typically the first department to open in the morning and the last to close at night. If members of the circulation staff can't help you directly, they should be able to point you to the person or office that can.

Reference

The **reference**, or **information, desk** is staffed by librarians specially trained in the use of information resources. They can help you with virtually every step of the research process. Most libraries now have some form of virtual presence, enabling you to chat, e-mail, and otherwise work directly with a librarian via the Internet. Many reference librarians have advanced subject degrees, enabling them to provide deeper insight into a given topic or discipline. Some librarians are even assigned to work with specific assignments, classes, and departments, giving them excellent insights into what's expected and what's needed to do a good job. The best thing? All the assistance they provide is free!

Interlibrary Loan

It is impossible for any library to have every source of information. But don't overlook potential sources of information simply because your library does not provide direct access to them. As the name suggests, if your library doesn't have the item you want, it may be available to you via **inter-library loan** (**ILL**). ILL enables you to acquire books and articles from other libraries. Delivery times are increasingly fast. So, in the end, although it may take a while longer to get the items you want through ILL, you may save yourself hours of research by having those sources available to you.

Instruction

Most libraries offer some form of **instruction** in the use of library and other information resources and services. Many times instructors will ask a librarian to speak with their students about resources they might use to complete assignments for the course. Other times librarians offer workshops or one-on-one sessions in which they teach you about some aspect of the research process. If there is no formal instruction at your library, most reference librarians are more than happy to teach you how to search for and use information more effectively. As noted, you can simply approach a librarian for assistance at the reference desk or schedule a one-on-one appointment to discuss your specific needs.

What Is a Librarian?

It is a common misconception that everyone who works in a library is a librarian. Many of the people you see working in a library are student workers or support staff. A librarian is an individual trained in the use of information and other technologies. Traditionally, this training involves completion of a one- to two-year program of study resulting in a master's degree in library science. However, the explosion of technology has necessitated changes to many curricula. As a result, many library science programs are embedded into, have merged with, or have completely evolved into information science programs. As noted, many academic librarians also have a master's degree (or higher) in a field of interest. As a result, they may be the library's specialists on particular topics.

There are many types of librarians. At small libraries, librarians often have multiple duties, whereas at large libraries, librarians may be more specialized. A **reference librarian** is specifically trained to assist you with virtually every aspect of the research process. In this respect, he or she is perhaps the most valuable asset your library has to offer you. Reference librarians typically staff a reference desk where they answer questions posed by library users. Most librarians are intellectually curious and have a genuine and sincere desire to help you if they can.

How Can a Reference Librarian Help?

Research is challenging. It can be frustrating. Struggling to find the best resources can take time, effort, and lots of patience. Learning how to acquire the right information can require even more. Reference librarians can help. They work with information and information resources every day. Many work directly with faculty members to create meaningful research assignments, and as a result, they typically know what's expected for your assignment. Whether you need help developing your topic, have questions about a citation style, or are looking for suggestions about possible resources and search strategies, reference librarians are there to assist. Although research might be new for you, it is what librarians are trained to do.

Librarians are uniquely qualified to help because they know the questions, they know what's available, and they know what search strategies work.

Librarians Know the Questions

Picture yourself in an introductory psychology class of thirty students. It's likely that a good number of those students have concerns and questions about research similar to yours. Now, imagine ten sections of that course being taught each semester. Further, imagine a librarian working with that course for ten years. If even just two students per class per semester ask the same question, that means the librarian has answered it two hundred times! In short, librarians know what instructors expect, and they work all the time to resolve student research crises.

Librarians Know What's Available

Many libraries provide access to dozens or even hundreds of electronic information resources and search tools. Names like Agricola and JSTOR, though, typically mean little to a researcher unless she has used such tools before. Librarians will work with you to find the most appropriate information resource(s) for your need. Moreover, if they can't find it locally, they have ways of acquiring books and articles from other libraries.

Librarians Know What Search Strategies Work

Let's say you are looking for books on the First World War. If your search produces no matching results, will you assume you need to adjust your search, or will you simply think that your library doesn't have any books on World War I? The former, it is hoped. Because every resource is different, what works in one search may or may not work in another. Librarians can help you discover what went wrong and can suggest various search strategies to address the problem.

Librarians Can't Know Everything

Just because librarians work with information and technology every day doesn't mean they are always able to help. Libraries are increasingly seen as access points to information, productivity software, and course software. Naturally everyone is different, and some librarians will know more about some resources than others. Just because a piece of software is loaded or a resource is available in the library doesn't mean every librarian will be familiar with it or know how to use it. Many types and varieties of information and information resources exist, and it is impossible for any one person to be aware of and know how to use all of them. When a librarian can't answer your question, he or she should be able to refer you to a colleague or other resource that can.

Selecting a Librarian

Essentially any librarian should be able to assist you with an introductory research assignment. That said, when approaching a librarian for assistance, many students select the one who has helped them in the past, the one with whom they feel most comfortable, or the **subject specialist**—the librarian with specific knowledge of the subject being researched. Unfortunately, as a new researcher, you won't know which librarian is best suited to your needs. Also, you often may not have a choice. For example, there may simply be only one librarian at your library or only one librarian available at the time you need assistance. In instances where you don't have a choice or your preferred librarian isn't available, you need to find a way to establish some form of working relationship.

When you do have a choice, here are some suggestions:

- Try coming to the library at different times. This gives you the chance to work with more than one librarian in order to determine which one you like working with the best.

- Communication is not a one-way street. Select a librarian who listens to you but who answers your questions in a way you understand and can apply.

- Although it's not always possible, selecting a librarian with knowledge matching your research needs and interests or one who has worked with students on the same assignment in the past can be an incredible advantage. Many times this will be the librarian who provides instruction to your class or who serves as liaison to the class or department. If you're not sure who is the most appropriate librarian to help you, explain your needs and ask who might be the best librarian to help you.

- Don't feel uncomfortable going to more than one librarian for help. Some librarians are better qualified in some areas or have more experience answering certain questions than others. Others are simply easier to communicate with. You need to find the one with whom you are most likely to experience success and with whom you're most comfortable working.

- Once you find a librarian you like working with, you can always schedule an appointment to meet with him or her individually.

A Note about Virtual Reference Services

As noted earlier in this chapter, libraries provide a growing amount and variety of virtual assistance. The forms such assistance can take are as many and as varied as the technologies that make it available. Some of the more common forms include recorded instruction sessions and online answers to frequently asked questions.

An increasingly common service is **virtual reference**, enabling students to get assistance with their research by working with a librarian online. Though this service is often geared toward students enrolled in online courses or who otherwise have difficulty getting to campus, many on-campus students use it as well. At the low end, you type a question and the librarian responds. At the high end, you may be able to engage a librarian directly via chat using text, voice, or some combination thereof. Too, many libraries provide live video so you can actually see whom you're chatting with.

However, providing assistance virtually poses a number of unique challenges for librarians and students alike. Not the least of these is that everyone has different technologies, operating systems, and software. As a result, the screens and functionalities of any two individuals' technologies often make it difficult to communicate meaningfully. For example, a librarian using a desktop system may have difficulty explaining how to use a resource to a student using a smartphone. Because of its smaller screen and other limitations, the smartphone may lack many of the features seen by the librarian. When speaking on the phone or via chat (and even more so with text), it's easy to misunderstand or misinterpret what's said. Slow typists, typographical errors, and the use of online jargon familiar to one person (e.g., TTYL) and not to the other only compound the difficulty.

Bottom line? If you live close enough to your institution, an in-person consultation is always preferred as it will generally be more productive and far less time-consuming in the long run than a virtual experience. Still, if a one-on-one visit isn't possible, be patient when using virtual services.

❓ REFLECTIONS

- Make a visit to the library. If you are at a large institution that has multiple libraries, start with the general undergraduate library. Spend time walking around and try to determine what you don't know about the library and the research process.

- Before asking specific questions, though, consider the following:

  ‣ Find out if your library offers tours, workshops, or other types of orientation sessions. If so, sign up for the topic(s) with which you need assistance. These activities should provide answers to many of your questions.

▸ If you're unable to participate in such activities or if an orientation isn't enough or doesn't give you the answers you want, identify a librarian. That is, don't ask a student worker or your friend for answers.

▸ Ask the librarian you've identified if he can spend ten to fifteen minutes answering your questions. Most librarians will be willing to do so if they're not too busy helping others. If the librarian you've asked isn't able to help you, he will certainly be able to direct you to someone who can.

- If you aren't sure what to ask, here are some common questions beginning researchers often have:

  ▸ Where do I sign out, return, and renew books?

  ▸ How do I access library search tools (e.g., indexes) and other resources for locating articles?

  ▸ What instruction do librarians provide on different aspects of the research process?

  ▸ Which resources are available, and how do I access them when I'm not in the library?

  ▸ When is the library open?

  ▸ When is a librarian available to provide me with assistance?

  ▸ What library services am I most likely to need and use as a first-time researcher?

- Of the four main types of libraries—academic, public, school, and special—visit two and note the similarities and differences in their layout, resources, and services.

- Share your research assignment with a librarian to determine some initial starting points for your research.

CHAPTER 4

Understanding Your Assignment

．．

For a variety of reasons (not the least of which is that your grade will be based on it), it is important for you to completely understand your assignment. Without understanding your assignment, you will not know what type or types of information you need to acquire, how many sources you're to use, and more. That is, the better you understand your assignment and your instructor's expectations, the easier it will be to conduct the research and complete your assignment.

Grading

To better understand your assignment, first look at how it will be graded. After all, that's one of the primary reasons you're doing this assignment in the first place. Some instructors will simply require the final paper. Along with a final paper, though, many instructors may require a series of smaller, related assignments that may or may not be graded. For example, before your assignment is even due, you may need to submit an outline of sources and search strategies you intend to use. The grade you receive on each of these other assignments may be incorporated into the overall grade you will receive for your term paper, or it may be calculated separately.

Inherent Value

Understanding how your term paper will be assessed—knowing the **inherent value** of each component—will help you to determine how much time and effort to put into each part of the assignment. Instructors each have their own scale, often assigning more points to the element or elements they feel are most significant or important. The following example uses common grading elements to illustrate how a term paper worth 100 points might be scored. In this example, writing well and following assignment guidelines are important. However, clearly this instructor's emphasis is more on the research elements (items 1 through 3: 75 percent) than on the mechanics of the paper (items 4 through 6: 25 percent).

1. Presence of a convincing, clearly articulated argument—25 points
2. Presence of adequate and appropriate support—25 points
3. Evidence of analysis of your topic—25 points
4. Correct and effective writing, including correct grammar and spelling—15 points
5. Properly cited sources—5 points
6. Evidence that assignment expectations were met—5 points

Relative Value

You also need to pay attention to how much your paper is worth relative to other assignments for the class—the paper's **relative value**. Because of the amount of work involved, term papers typically constitute a major part of a semester's grade. It is not uncommon that your term paper will be worth 25 to 50 percent of your overall final grade. For the sake of argument, let's say that your instructor counts your term paper as 50 percent of your overall course grade. Translated, this means this one assignment is worth as much as all the other course assignments combined. It also means you should be spending as much (or more) time on your term paper as on your other assignments for the course.

Assignment Elements

When conducting research, finding appropriate types and amounts of information is certainly important. However, to place your research in context and to use your time and effort effectively, you need to be aware of your instructor's various expectations for your finished product. The degree to which you understand these elements plays a key role in helping you to manage your time, focus your research, and otherwise complete your paper in an effective and efficient manner.

Deadlines

One of the first things to look at is your assignment's deadlines. This doesn't mean just finding out when the final paper is due. You may be expected to submit elements of the project *before* the final paper. A preliminary research plan, a list of sources you intend to use, and a rough draft are common. By knowing what needs to be completed when, you can budget your time and effort more effectively, as discussed in chapter 2.

Type of Term Paper

There are many types of term papers. Some instructors will assign you a specific type of term paper; others will allow you to select the type you wish to write. By understanding the type of paper you will be writing, you will be able to better identify the type of information you need to search for and acquire. Whichever type of paper you are assigned (or choose to write), be sure it is aligned with your purpose statement (see chapter 5) and vice versa.

The following sections highlight some key activities and emphases associated with each of the three main types of term papers you are likely to encounter at this point in your academic career. As noted, you should select the type of term paper that is best suited to achieving your research objectives.

Descriptive/Informative

The **descriptive/informative** type of term paper . . .

- Describes the nature of a topic
- Details key attributes of a topic
- Enables the researcher to acquire a deeper knowledge of a topic or issue

You may or may not be asked to include personal opinions and perspectives.

Argumentative/Opinion

An **argumentative/opinion** type of term paper . . .

- Takes a stand on a topic and justifies it with evidence (the stand taken may or may not be one with which you agree)

- Provides strong evidence and effective arguments for (or against) a particular idea
- Must deal with a topic that has a counterpoint or counterargument
- Presents factual information in a logical manner
- Typically discusses both sides—pro and con—of the issue

Compare/Contrast

The **compare/contrast** type of term paper...

- Describes similarities and differences between two or more topics or concepts
- Supports a thesis

Date of Information

Determine whether there is a date restriction on the information you can use. Although many instructors don't care, others do, and they may allow you to use only information published within a certain period. To get a feeling for how people were responding at the time, a history professor, for example, might want you to use only sources from 1935 to 1950 to write a paper on World War II. On the other hand, because current information is so important, a nursing instructor may allow you to use only sources published within the past five years.

Citation Style

Each discipline has a preferred style and format for **citing** sources in a consistent manner. The social sciences, for example, tend to use APA (American Psychological Association) style. Other common styles include MLA (Modern Language Association) and Chicago. The primary differences among these and other styles concern what information is required, how it's to be formatted, and where it's to be placed. Some instructors will prescribe which citation style you are to use. Others will not care and will let you decide. If you are given a choice, it is highly recommended that you choose the style associated with your chosen discipline because you are likely to use it for the remainder of your academic career and beyond. If you do not have the appropriate style guide, check with your library or your instructor to see if you can borrow a copy.

Length

One of the most common questions students ask about term papers is, "How long does it have to be?" Many instructors will answer, "As long as it needs to be." That may sound flippant; however, every class and every instructor have different expectations. As a result, there is no single way to answer this question that will apply to every paper. Some considerations that affect the length of your final paper include the following:

Assigned length: Some instructors will impose a page limit or a range of pages. A limit of ten to fifteen pages is fairly common.

Style: Because everyone's writing style varies, some writers may use more (or fewer) words than others.

Format: Some instructors will specify the margins, fonts, line spacing, and other formatting to be used.

Images/graphics: The inclusion of such components as charts, graphs, and pictures can quickly consume a lot of space. Be sure you understand what, if any, limit your instructor has placed on the number of images you can include, what size they are to be, and so on.

> Be aware that a "page" typically refers to a *full* page of content, not a partial page.
>
> Page requirements typically refer to *content pages only*. That is, such elements as title pages, tables of contents, and lists of references are usually not considered "pages" and do not count toward satisfying your page limit.

Sources

Source material can be one of the most confounding aspects of research for a beginner. Sifting through the sheer volume and variety of sources can be daunting. But when first-time researchers think of source material, there are a number of aspects they don't know about, tend to overlook, or simply do not consider important enough to worry about. However, be aware that overlooking these considerations can result in a lower grade if they are part of your assignment requirements. At the very least, ignoring them can result in a paper of lesser or poorer quality. The following sections highlight some of these key considerations.

Quantity

Some instructors may require you to use a minimum number of sources or a minimum number of a type of source. For example, you might be asked to use a minimum of ten sources, or you may be asked to use no fewer than three books, five articles, and two websites. When a number is not specified, it will be up to you to determine how many sources you need to complete your paper.

When selecting your own number of sources, obviously the quantity will vary by writing style, depth, topic, and other factors. A good rule of thumb is to use at least one to two sources per page of content. Thus, if you are to write a ten-page paper, you are likely to have ten to twenty sources, some of which you will use more than others. However, this doesn't mean you can't use one source multiple times, nor does it mean using one source for virtually every piece of information in your paper. Using multiple sources gives you the opportunity to present new content, to incorporate new perspectives, and to write with variety, all of which will make your paper stronger in the long run.

Format

Information is available in many different formats. Books, periodicals, and websites are three of the most common. However, every instructor has different expectations about formats. Although books, articles, and websites may be the most common information formats you will be using, you might also use a government publication, a dissertation, or information from any of a number of other formats in compiling your research. That said, your instructor may place restrictions on what you can and cannot use. For example, many instructors specify the number of websites, if any, you are permitted to use. Whether your instructor specifies the types of sources or not, realize that good research typically uses a mix of books, articles, and other sources of information. How to determine which sources to use and when to pick one over another are discussed more in chapter 10. For now, in terms of understanding your assignment, you need to determine what (if any) restrictions your instructor has placed on the format of the sources you are supposed to use (or not use).

Type

In discussing sources or conducting research, you might hear or come across the term *primary source* or *primary research* as opposed to *secondary source* or *secondary research*. As discussed earlier, data come from, and research is built on, both types. Moreover, secondary research often involves the use of primary source material. However, with *very rare* exceptions, when you are generating an undergraduate term paper, you do so by conducting secondary research. But what does that mean?

Primary Research

Primary research involves original, firsthand experience in which you are personally conducting and reporting on an experiment or research topic. **Primary source** material typically includes such items as speeches, diaries, interviews, live performances, original reports, autobiographies, and eyewitness accounts and observations.

> Example: You experiment to determine the effectiveness of drug X in curing autism.

Secondary Research

Secondary research reports on, synthesizes, and interprets both primary and secondary research data and, as a result, is more subject to errors of interpretation, emphasis, memory, and personal bias. Among others, examples of secondary sources include books, biographies, histories (not autobiographical), magazine articles, newspapers, and news reports.

> Example: You read and report on information you find in articles, books, and other sources about the ability of drug X to cure autism.

Audience

Information is written and published for three main audiences. Though these levels are most often associated with periodicals, they can also be loosely applied to books and other sources of information. Your instructor may or may not specify which level or levels you are allowed to use. Generally speaking, though, particularly in your upper-level courses, you should strive to use sources that represent scholarly, academic treatment of a subject. Specific distinctions between each of the following are presented in greater detail in chapter 7.

Popular

For lack of a better term, the most basic level of information is published at the popular level and is geared to the general population. The information is written and presented at a nonacademic level with the intent of being understandable to the broadest cross section of the population as possible. Although some **popular publications** are focused, most contain general information on a variety of topics. Books and magazines found at supermarkets and bookstores generally contain this sort of information. Many websites are geared toward providing this sort of information as well.

Scholarly/Academic

Though not exclusively, most **scholarly**, or **academic**, **publications** focus on a particular topic or range of related topics. They are usually referred to as *journals*. Information appearing in these publications is generally produced by individuals working in a field or occupation related to the topic. As a result, the information tends to be more reliable and informative than that in consumer-level publications dealing with the same topic. It is possible for someone with a strong background or interest in a topic to have work published. Perhaps your local jeweler has an interest in animals. She may have an article published in a journal focusing on biology. However, it is far more likely that the majority of contributors to the journal will have experience with or work in a field directly related to biology, such as high school biology teaching or veterinary medicine. The same would be true of scholarly books on biology.

Refereed/Peer-Reviewed

All refereed or peer-reviewed journals are scholarly or academic but not the reverse. Information in **peer-reviewed**, or **refereed**, **publications** is *very* focused and is reviewed by a group of *peers*—people highly knowledgeable in the subject—before it is published. The peers act as referees in that they are familiar with the topic and know its rules. This enables them to critically evaluate content for accuracy, timeliness, and relevance, among other qualities. Because it is reviewed by individuals in the know, information contained in these publications is seen as being of the highest caliber. Although scholarly and academic works are also reviewed, the reviewers may or may not have any experience with the topic. Their main focus is to determine if the information is appropriate for their publication. Telling the difference between the two is discussed in chapter 7.

> Whatever level of publication you use, you must be able to understand what you read. If you can't, you shouldn't use material from that source. For example, the *Journal of Orthopsychiatry* might have great articles, but if you don't know what orthopsychiatry is or means, it's unlikely you'll be able to understand much of the content contained in the journal.

❓ REFLECTIONS

- Ask your professor for a copy of a successfully completed term paper in order to get a better sense of what's expected.
- In addition to the written requirements for your paper, are there also requirements for either (a) images or (b) a PowerPoint (or similar) presentation?
- Look at the assignments listed on each of your course syllabi this term.
    a. How many involve research?
    b. Determine the inherent and relative values of each assignment for each course.
    c. Develop a prioritized list (with deadlines) for the items in part b.

CHAPTER 5

Selecting a Research Topic

B ecause it is the foundation on which your research, your term paper, and (ultimately) your grade rest, picking a topic is arguably the most important aspect of the research process. And it is also the one with which many first-time researchers struggle.

What Is a Topic?

A topic is more than just a few terms and ideas you'll use to conduct your search for information. You also need to think about your topic in context. For example, if you're doing a term paper on dress codes in schools, you'll find a lot of information. But are you focusing on elementary or secondary school? Private or public? The teachers' perspective or the students'? By placing your topic into a context, you'll not only focus your research, you'll have a framework for determining the relevance of the information your research generates.

> Some of the key factors to consider when placing your topic in context include age, gender, geography, perspective, time period, race, and location (e.g., hospital versus school).

Picking Your Destination

For starters, think of choosing a topic as if you were traveling through a big city looking for a restaurant that serves fish-on-a-stick. Admittedly, if you wander around long enough, you'll eventually find the restaurant. However, this method obviously isn't very effective as you're likely to spend a lot of time going down the wrong streets, many of which will turn out to be dead ends. Instead, before starting off, if you know the name and address of the restaurant that serves fish-on-a-stick, you can go there much more directly and quickly.

Picking a topic is no different. Think of it as your destination. The more you know up front about what you want to research, the more focused and successful your research is likely to be. For example, rather than wandering randomly, you could get a map or ask someone to help direct you to where you want to go.

Let Your Topic Guide Your Research

This is the first rule for choosing (and staying with) your topic. Rather than letting their topic guide their research, beginning researchers often make the mistake of letting their research guide their topic. That is, they may not have a clear topic in mind or may experience difficulty finding the information they want. As a result, they start their research by browsing until they find a topic that seems to have a lot of information. They then choose that as the topic of their research.

Successful researchers, though, use their topic to guide their research. They spend time at the beginning carefully choosing a topic, developing questions they'd like to answer, and generating possible search terms and strategies for finding the information they want. When they encounter difficulties, they don't change their topic; they change the way in which they seek information.

Methods for Topic Selection

There are three ways in which you can pick a topic for your term paper.

Predetermined

You won't always have the luxury of being able to pick your own research topic. For any of a number of reasons, your instructor may assign you a topic. Often it's done simply as a way of guaranteeing variety. Other times, instructors assign a range of topics as a way of focusing students on a particular subject or aspect of the class. For example, you may be assigned to do a paper on a historical event before 1980. Although your instructor has set the theme, it will be up to you to decide which particular event you wish to research.

Menu

In this scenario, you pick a topic from a list of topics supplied by your instructor. The topics usually revolve around the central themes of the course, or they may be random.

Open

Many instructors allow you to pick your own topic. A common limit, if any, is to restrict you to researching a topic relevant to the course. To ensure variety, your instructor might also prohibit you from selecting commonly researched topics, such as gun control, abortion, and the death penalty.

Some instructors allow you to pick the topic you want to research but will want to approve it before they allow you to begin your research. This is done for a variety of reasons, the most common of which is to demonstrate that you understand your topic and where you want to go with it. In this context, saying you want to do a paper on "the Revolution," for example, isn't likely to be approved. It's simply not detailed enough. After meeting with your professor, though, you might refine your topic specifically to the American Revolution and even further to causes behind it or living conditions in the military camps or weapons used.

Selecting a Researchable Topic

Just because you have a great idea or a topic that really motivates you to learn more doesn't mean it's researchable. Students often pick a topic that is too broad or too narrow. Sometimes there is insufficient information on their topic, or the information isn't readily available. Other times, they pick a topic that can't sustain their interest. In order for you to proceed through the research process efficiently and productively, a researchable topic should possess as many of the following characteristics as possible:

- Sufficient, relevant information is available from appropriate sources.
- Information is readily accessible and easy to acquire.
- The information is based on facts rather than opinions, values, or beliefs.
- The topic sustains your interest.
- The topic meets or exceeds assignment requirements.
- The topic has a clear focus, allowing you to analyze, argue, or explain.
- The topic is comprehensible to you as you read about it.

Nonresearchable Topics

Despite all that you've just read, there may come a time when you need to decide whether to continue pursuing your topic. Among other problems, you may have trouble finding information or may be finding too much. Before you change your topic, though, it's highly recommended that you talk with your instructor or a librarian. Often the problems associated with a topic aren't necessarily with the topic itself but with the way a student is thinking about or trying to discover information about the topic. This is particularly true with lower-level, introductory courses. Sharing your ideas often generates new ideas or pathways to explore.

If you're struggling with your topic, you should be asking yourself the following questions. If you answer yes to any of them, you may have a nonresearchable topic. Again, if so, don't wait to talk with your instructor or a librarian about what to do next.

- Is my topic too broad or too narrow?
- Does my topic rely on opinions, beliefs, or values rather than facts?
- Does my topic allow me to inject my own analysis or personal insights?

- Is the topic too recent to have sufficient information available?
- Is the limited amount of information on my topic due to the fact that it's a local topic without broad appeal?

Sources for Topics

A topic can emerge from just about anywhere. Personal experiences, classroom lectures, and simple browsing of articles, books, websites, and other information sources are common starting points. At the very least, your topic should be one that interests you or with which you have some experience. Many times, this interest or experience can be combined with some aspect of your major program of study. For example, an education major might choose a topic related to dress codes because of his experiences with them in high school. Similarly, you could explore a topic that is related to your friends or family. If you have a relative who died from lung cancer, for example, you may opt to research how a parent's lung cancer (or terminal illness in general) impacts other members of the family.

☑ TIPS

- Because research often involves multiple disciplines, think about your topic from different angles and perspectives. You could look at dress codes, for example, from a teacher's, parent's, principal's, or student's point of view.
- Start with a subject with which you're familiar and expand on it by browsing sources related to your topic for additional names, terms, concepts, and more.
- Talk with your advisor or someone in the field who knows about areas of interest to you.
- Select an issue or topic related to your course or major program of study.
- Pick a topic about which you have a strong opinion or which is controversial.

Brainstorming for Ideas

Many students combine one or more of the preceding strategies with brainstorming to generate a topic. Brainstorming involves spending a few minutes writing down every thought and idea that come to mind. You could start with a news story that captured your attention that day, an issue you faced with your significant other, or a concern you have as a student athlete—anything. The only rule is that no idea is too far-fetched. At this stage, the focus is on generating ideas.

Then, once you've completed your list, set it aside for a bit and come back to it later. At that time, begin to focus your list and clarify your topic. Whether your list turns out to be big or small, it's okay. If it's small, that may be a sign that you don't know enough about the topic to begin researching it. But don't automatically cast the topic aside. If you really like it, spend some time becoming more familiar with it and then decide accordingly. On the other hand, if your list is too large, use it to generate additional ideas or to find a common, manageable theme that you can research. In both cases, if an idea doesn't produce any tangible direction or approaches, cross it off your list.

There are many brainstorming techniques you might try depending on your needs. Three such techniques follow.

Freewriting

When most people think of brainstorming, they're thinking of **freewriting**, wherein you write down anything and everything that comes to mind. The whole point is to help you overcome being self-conscious about yourself and your topic. When you freewrite, you're more likely to be more open with your thoughts and ideas. You can set a time limit (maybe twenty minutes) or a page limit (perhaps two to three pages) and then stop when you reach that limit. While writing, don't worry about style or whether you're babbling. Even if you think you're not saying anything valuable, the important thing is to keep writing whatever comes to mind. When you're done, you'll have a lot of unusable content. But you're also likely to discover some themes, insights, and so on that you hadn't thought of before you began and that you can use to develop your topic.

Clustering/Mapping

With the **clustering**, or **mapping**, technique, you write down random words, concepts, names, and so on associated with your topic. When you've finished, you impose order by circling related terms and connecting them with a line. To help show related clusters, you might use colored pencils or markers. Say you wish to research arguments for and against gun control, specifically with respect to keeping guns out of the hands of criminals. Though in no way comprehensive, figure 5.1 provides an example of how

FIGURE 5.1

Topic Clustering/Mapping

you might start to map your topic using this technique. Shapes and shading are used to indicate subtopics and details. Here, dark shapes—uses, users, and types—represent broad subtopics while lighter shapes, such as civilians and law enforcement, are used to show further specificity. You might wish to use additional arrows, colors, or other techniques to map various clusters (or parts of clusters) to one another. For example, you might want to indicate that civilians use guns for hunting and for self-protection.

Cubing

Just as a cube has six sides, **cubing** is a technique requiring you to examine your topic from six different perspectives. Common "sides" include the terms *describe*, *compare*, *associate*, *analyze*, *apply*, and *argue* (for or against). When you've completed your cube, look for relationships. For example, do some ideas seem to go together, or do some repeat themselves? By looking at your topic in this way, you are likely to gain a deeper understanding of your topic as well as insight into how you'll work with it throughout the research process. Figure 5.2 illustrates cubing. As you look at the image, you can apply the following example text to each of the cube's sides. After doing so, it should be easier to visualize various relationships, such as making comparisons and analyzing the technologies described.

Example of Cubing

Topic: Are people spending too much time online and not enough time communicating face-to-face with others and maintaining relationships?

Describe: Technology is everywhere, and more and more individuals are using technologies such as texting and social media to interact and communicate with others.

Compare: Because technology is impacting society on a number of levels, comparisons can be drawn between the use of technology at, say, work, school, and home.

Associate: Social media, interpersonal communication, social aspects of technology.

FIGURE 5.2

Cubing

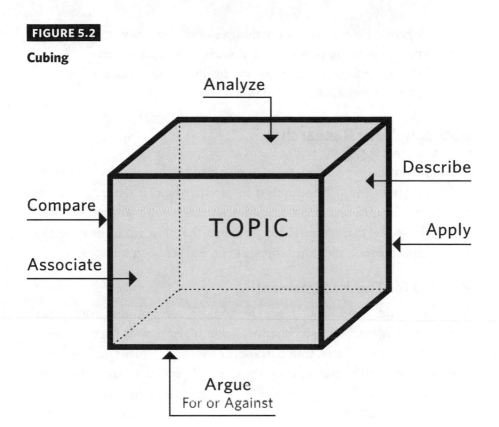

Analyze: Does the use of technology enhance or compromise our ability to effectively communicate and interact with individuals in person?

Apply: Technology makes communicating easier but typically lacks the visual and auditory cues that help us to better understand what's being communicated.

Argue for/against:

> *For*: Technology gives shy individuals a means to express themselves. You can talk with people you wouldn't otherwise have a chance to meet. People from other countries as well as those with different lifestyles and from different cultures are good examples. Communication with someone isn't time or space dependent.

Against: People do and say things online that they would not do or say in person. Text alone is easy to misunderstand or misinterpret. Many use online communication to avoid awkward confrontations.

Focusing Your Research

Having identified a starting point in terms of your topic, the next step is to identify how you will focus your research around it. That is, you need to identify the purpose, direction, and perspective you plan to take. This is accomplished by three interrelated elements that flow from the general to the specific: purpose statement, hypothesis, and research questions.

Purpose (or Thesis) Statement

Your topic and, hence, your research should revolve around your paper's purpose statement, or thesis. Because it summarizes your paper in one to two declarative sentences, your purpose, or thesis, statement indicates what you hope to achieve through your research. It serves as the axis around which your research should revolve. Although it will not necessarily be a discrete part or distinct section of your final paper, it is an essential aspect of every research project. When a reader has read your paper, she should be able to indicate the degree to which you successfully accomplished your purpose. To that end, your thesis statement should . . .

- Explain the topic of your paper
- Discuss the objectives or purpose of your research

> In drafting a purpose statement, don't presuppose an answer. "This paper will explore the positive impact of drinking wine each day" presupposes that there is a positive impact. Instead, consider " . . . the impact of drinking wine each day" or, even more specifically, " . . . the health effects that drinking wine has on pregnant women." With the latter, you aren't already assuming the impact is positive. Your research will guide you to that conclusion (or not).

- Outline the main points you'll be discussing
- Identify the perspective you'll be taking on your topic

Purpose, or thesis, statements often begin with wording such as the following:

"The purpose of this paper is to ..."

"This paper will discuss ..."

"In this paper, I will explore/discuss/argue ..."

Purpose statements can be weak or strong. The stronger your statement, the easier it will be to focus your research efforts. The following is an example of a weak purpose statement:

This paper will discuss eating disorders.

Why is it weak? The statement is simply much too broad and vague to be useful. For example, which eating disorder or disorders will you be discussing? Which aspects of eating disorders will you be researching? For example, will you be examining causes or treatments or history? Or, will you be focusing on a particular category of people, such as females or teenage girls? Admittedly, a thesis statement can't answer all such questions. However, at the very least, it should provide the specific direction and perspective you plan to take with your topic.

Now, let's try to make the statement stronger by addressing some of these questions. Yes, it could still be improved. However, notice the strength it gains by addressing the specific purpose, focus, and perspective of the paper.

The purpose of this research paper is to discuss effective treatment options for teenage girls diagnosed with bulimia.

Hypothesis

A **hypothesis** reflects a perspective you take on your thesis. It is a prediction about what you believe your research will reveal. Your hypothesis is not set in stone. Like your topic, it may evolve as new information becomes available. However, it focuses your topic by addressing a single aspect. For this example, your hypothesis might be stated like this:

Some treatments for bulimia, including nutritional counseling and cognitive behavioral therapy, are more effective than others.

Or this:

Some teenage female bulimia patients respond better to treatment with cognitive behavioral therapy than to other treatments.

Your instructor may (or may not) require you to submit a hypothesis. Depending on your purpose and the type of paper you're writing (see chapter 4), your research should reflect information that supports your hypothesis and overall purpose or that counters arguments against your hypothesis and purpose, or both.

Research Questions

Research questions are specific questions you hope to answer through your research. They narrow your purpose statement into the fundamental questions inherent in your overall topic and will form the basis for your paper. Two research questions for the preceding topic might be these:

Why do some bulimia treatments work better with older teenagers than with younger ones?

What role does peer mentoring play in the bulimia treatment process?

Accepting Uncertainty

Realize that you may need or want to evolve your topic as you learn more about it. As you gather more information, you might find a new path to follow or develop a perspective on your topic you hadn't thought of before. This doesn't necessarily mean you have to change your topic. It just means focusing or redirecting your research slightly to pursue new lines of information. For example, you may start researching head injuries to football players and conclude by presenting a historical overview of the evolution of football equipment over the past century. Although the specifics have changed, you're still researching a related topic based on what you've discovered, new interests, and so on.

Changing Your Topic

You should change your topic only as a last resort and only after consulting with your instructor or a librarian. Will there be times that you *want* to change your topic? Most definitely. Will there be times you *need* to change your topic? Sometimes, yes. In both cases, however, be sure you speak with your instructor before doing so. Among other things, there may be penalties for changing topics midstream. More than that, though, the problem may not be as much with your topic as it is with how you're approaching it or how you are searching for relevant information. Your instructor or a librarian should be able to give you some new ideas and perspectives to enable you to get past whatever hurdle you're encountering.

❓ REFLECTIONS

- Browse the table of contents, index, and a chapter of interest in one of your textbooks to identify a possible topic.

- Speak with a librarian to determine the location of books on a topic of interest to you and then browse the shelves for ideas.

- Select a topic from the following list and provide at least three perspectives and three related terms or ideas you could explore to narrow down and focus your topic. For example:

  Broad topic: gambling addiction

  Perspectives: business, gambler, casino owner, family members of gambling addicts, psychological

  Terms: table games, addictive personalities, slot machines, the psychology of gambling, lottery tickets, athletic contests, horse racing

  - Online social media
  - Substance abuse
  - Obesity
  - Terrorism
  - Cults
  - Superheroes
  - American Civil War
  - Illegal music downloads

- Indicate why each of the following is *not* a researchable topic.
    - ▸ God's views on hunting
    - ▸ The role of darkness in literature
    - ▸ The impact of football on the academic success of ninth grade boys at Philadelphia's ABC High School in 1957
    - ▸ Why blueberry pie tastes better than apple pie
- Identify how and why the following purpose statements are weak and rewrite them so that they are stronger.
    - ▸ The purpose of this paper is to detail the impact of drunk drivers.
    - ▸ This paper will discuss the effects of sleep deprivation.
    - ▸ In this paper, I will explore methods of math instruction.

CHAPTER 6

Locating Information Resources

· ·

Many researchers struggle with finding appropriate information because they do not have a clear understanding of how the information search tool they are using stores information. As a result, they have difficulty generating effective search strategies to find the information they are seeking. Therefore, before you begin looking for information on your topic, it is important for you to develop a working knowledge of how information is stored and accessed. This chapter examines some of the underlying terms and ideas associated with information formatting and storage. The following chapter will focus on selecting resources and on accessing information more effectively through specific research strategies and concepts.

What Is an Information Resource?
· ·
Source Materials

When you hear the term *information resource*, what comes to mind? If you are like most beginning researchers, you probably think of books, periodicals, and websites. These are certainly examples of information resources. They are the products of your research, the destination of your research journey if you will.

Each has strengths and weaknesses, as shown in figure 6.1, and good, effective research is likely to use information from all three types. Even so, you may use some types of sources more than others. For example, if your paper focuses on a topic over an extended period—the causes of World

War I, for example—you may rely more heavily on books than on periodicals because of their depth and breadth of coverage. Still, deciding which specific sources of information to use will be guided by your assignment needs and purpose statement.

FIGURE 6.1

Strengths and Weaknesses of Various Resource Types

Resource Type	Strengths	Weaknesses
Monograph *Published once or as a revision or continuation of an earlier work (e.g., 2nd Edition, Volume II)* *Examples: book, report, document, speech*	• Covers a topic in great detail, with greater context • Includes more complete information (e.g., long-term effects) • Has broader perspective • Often contains lists of references and other useful documents	• Because the lapse between writing and publishing can be significant, the information may not always be current • May cover only a single topic • Unless available in electronic format, you must either physically go to where the item is located or wait for interlibrary loan • Can take much time to read and review
Periodical *Published regularly (e.g., weekly, monthly, quarterly)* *Examples: magazine, journal, newspaper*	• Shorter and easier to read than a book • Newspapers are excellent for current events as well as local and regional issues and concerns • Because the lapse between writing and publishing is usually relatively short, the information tends to be very current and good for time-sensitive topics and stories • Can follow the evolution of a story closely over days or even weeks	• Professional journals often require a subscription (e.g., library) or a fee • Information is current but may be incomplete, lack context, or both • May lack depth except for the topic being discussed • May lack good indexing, making it difficult to locate articles of interest • Unless available in electronic format, you must either physically go to where the item is located or wait for interlibrary loan

Continued on next page

Resource Type	Strengths	Weaknesses
Web-Based Source *No standard for publishing—may be published once or updated regularly, completely at the discretion of the person or group generating the information* *Examples: website, electronic discussion list, news feed, blog*	• Great breadth and depth of information • Searching is relatively consistent and familiar to most people • Accessible wherever there is Internet access	• Information is often inaccurate, purposely biased, or out of date • Not arranged by subject • Sites disappear or alter without notice

Search Tools

The preceding, though, represents only one side of the information resource coin. The remainder of this chapter will discuss the other side—information search tools as the vehicles for getting you the materials you seek. That is, what are the tools, the discovery mechanisms, you will use to find books, periodicals, websites, and other types of information? As noted, the better you understand these tools and how they work, the more effective your searches will be. You will be using three main information search tools.

Catalogs

Many stores publish a catalog of the items they sell or make available to customers. The same is true of libraries. A library **catalog** (also called an **online public access catalog**, or **OPAC**) provides a way to determine if the library has the item you want. Most people think of using a library catalog to find books. But a library's catalog can also be used to search for periodicals, music, movies, and a whole lot more. Increasingly, catalogs contain links to electronic resources as well—resources not housed physically within the library but to which the library provides access.

Indexes

Although many use the terms *index* and *database* interchangeably, in reality, it is more appropriate to think of them as two distinct tools working together. Basically, whereas a **database** is a collection of organized information, an **index** points you to where the information can be found within the database. If you think of a book as a database (i.e., it contains the content), the index at the back points you to specific points of interest within the book. Here, the term *index* will be used to refer mainly to a tool that arranges periodical content in a searchable manner, such as by subject or author.

Search Engines

A **search engine** is a tool used to find information on the Internet. Although most people have used (or at least heard of) the search engine named Google, there are actually hundreds of search engines from which to choose. Some, like Google, are used for general searches of the Internet. Others can be used to search for specific types of Internet sites or for specific types of information. USA.gov, for example, is an excellent search engine to use if you want to find government information.

Anatomy of Search Tools

Information resources provide access to a vast amount of information. Although such things as vendor interfaces and how you search a resource will vary, the underlying way information is stored does not. Therefore, understanding how information is stored is a critical first step for developing an effective search strategy and for otherwise searching a given information resource more efficiently.

Books and Articles

When searching for books and articles, you are essentially searching records and fields for matches to whatever terms (or other search criteria) you have entered.

Records

A **record** represents all the data stored in a database about a particular item. For example, a record for a book is likely to contain such information as the book's title, author, publisher, year of publication, and so on. Every record within a given database will contain the same respective information and present it in the same, uniform manner. That is, if the information about the author appears first for book 1 in the database, it will appear first for all the other books in the database as well.

Fields

Each piece of information stored in a database record is stored in a **field**. That is, a field contains a specific type of information and is consistent for every record. Author information is stored in the author field, for example, not in the title field. The use of fields to focus and refine your searches is discussed in chapter 8.

Websites

Websites are not comprised of records or fields. Search engines essentially compile a database of websites. When you conduct a search for information on the Internet, the search engine searches for matches in its index of the websites in its database (versus searching the records and fields for matches). Keep in mind that the sheer volume of websites and the countless number of new sites produced every day make it impossible for any search engine to search the entire Internet. So, just as with other information tools, using one or more search engines to search the Internet will help to ensure you have found as much as you can on your topic. Keep in mind that you can search for books and periodicals on the Internet, but the results are not likely to be as relevant as a similar search of a catalog or index.

Access Issues
. . . .

Chapter 2 outlined some basic access considerations to be aware of before starting your research. Although a growing number of search tools are available twenty-four hours a day, many resources are not. Knowing which are available when can enable you to better manage your time.

When deciding how to conduct your research, there are three primary access issues to consider that may influence the tools you decide to use for your research (and when). Figure 6.2 summarizes these issues.

FIGURE 6.2

Strengths and Weaknesses of Various Access Types

Access Type	Strengths	Weaknesses
Remote *Accessible via any computer connected to the Internet*	Conduct research at any time of the day	May not have or know proper log-in or authorization Some resource features may not be available remotely Different browsers and devices may cause variations in display and functionality
Restricted *Whether available via the Internet or just locally, there are limits set on things such as who can use (e.g., faculty), when (e.g., after 5:00 p.m.), and number of simultaneous users*	Often provide access to highly specialized or very expensive resources	May have to wait until another user logs off May only be available at certain times of the day (e.g., off-peak hours, weekends) May not have the appropriate level of authorization (e.g., grad student, faculty) Typically have unique or additional access requirements
Physical *Available only in the library*	Lots of information is still accessible only in printed format	Requires you to go to the library to access the item

Unavailable Information Resources

The sheer volume of information that is available, cost, space requirements, and other factors make it impossible for any library to own or otherwise provide access to every book and article published. But that doesn't mean you should give up hope. For books, check other libraries in the area for a copy. Before making the trip to get the item, check online or call to see if the item is available for lending.

If there are not other libraries in the area or you are not able to get to one, speak with a librarian about a service called interlibrary loan (ILL). When you want a book your library does not have, your librarian will locate other libraries that do. You then pick up and return the book at your library.

For articles, ILL is even more straightforward. In rare instances, you may still be sent a printed copy, but the overwhelming number of articles you request are sent to you via e-mail, often the same day as your request.

❓ REFLECTIONS

- Speak with a librarian about interlibrary loan (ILL) and similar services to learn how to acquire books and articles not directly available at your library.
- Examine a book, an article, and a website on a topic of interest and note similarities and differences in depth of coverage, the date the information was published, and so on.
- What is the name of your library's catalog?
- If your school has more than one library, which is the most appropriate to your research need?
- What is the procedure for logging in to your library's information resources from off-site?

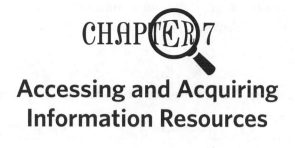

Accessing and Acquiring
Information Resources

· ·

N ow that you have a grasp of the basics of how information is stored, it is time to talk about specific things you need to consider when selecting a search tool to find information. Access to indexes and other information search tools is typically provided via links on a library's home page. An alphabetical list or a list arranged by the primary content focus of the search tool (e.g., biology, nursing, art) is common. Some libraries may also have separate links to search tools for finding books and those for finding articles. Even so, deciding which specific search tool(s) to use can be a significant challenge. It can also lead to unsatisfactory results and undue frustration.

Information Formats
· · · · · · · · · · · · · · · · · · · ·

As noted earlier, successful time management is a central element to conducting effective research. With that in mind, one of the first things you should consider as you begin searching is the format of the information you are seeking. A growing number of items—especially articles—are available electronically in **full-text**. This means the entire item is electronically available for downloading and printing. However, if you focus on only **electronic full-text**, you will be eliminating countless other possible sources of information.

Library-Based Content

Figure 7.1 summarizes the three most common formats of information found in libraries and lists the main advantage and disadvantage of each.

Advantages and Disadvantages of Various Formats

Medium	Advantage	Disadvantage
Print *Item available in print*	Most common and familiar format	Requires you to be where the item is located
Electronic Full-Text (or Full-Text) *Complete item available electronically or digitally*	Typically available remotely	Not every printed resource has an electronic version
Microforms *Item available on microfilm, microfiche, microcard, or microprint*	Provide access to information often not found in any other format	Require use of specialized technology to read and to print

✓ TIPS

- Instead of arbitrarily eliminating a format from your research, budget your time to accommodate all formats so as not to overlook key sources of information.

- Because printed items and items on **microforms** (e.g., **microfiche**, **microcard**, **microfilm**, **ultrafiche**) require you to be physically present, you should budget extra time to acquire or copy these resources. Conversely, because they are available at any time, consider focusing on electronic resources last or when you have only a limited amount of time.

Web-Based Content

One key format not mentioned previously is web-based content, which is essentially any information that can be found on the Web. Because a search of the Internet is familiar to many students and because such searches typically yield results, many people are conditioned to go there first for information. This is not necessarily a bad strategy. At the very least, it can be a great way to identify key names, dates, and other information associated with a topic. Too, there is a lot of good information to be found on the Web that cannot be found anywhere else or found as easily. However, there are trade-offs. For example, the vast majority of websites are not monitored for accuracy, currency, and other criteria necessary for good research. It is not uncommon to find inaccurate content or content that disappears. What to watch for and how to evaluate web content will be discussed further in chapter 10. For now, as with any information format, remember that it is ultimately up to you to decide whether or not web-based information meets your information need.

Depth of Content

When selecting sources, choosing an appropriate level of content is very important. Simply put, the best source in the world isn't any good if you are not able to understand what you are reading. In that regard, it is helpful to note the difference between the two content emphases of resources. Depending on where you are in the research process and how much you already know about your topic, you may find it useful to use one or both types.

General Resources

As the name implies, the focus of general resources is broad. They are "an inch deep and a mile wide." That means they cover a variety of topics and subject areas but none in any great detail. These resources are good for browsing, developing a working familiarity with your topic (including key terms, dates, and names), and otherwise getting started. However, because they are general, you may have difficulty finding much (if any) information that's relevant to your topic and purpose.

Examples:

American Heritage Dictionary of the English Language

World Book Encyclopedia

Academic Search Complete (general database for articles)

Subject-Specific Resources

By contrast, subject-specific information sources are "an inch wide and a mile deep." They focus on one topic or one aspect of a topic in great detail. As a result, they are generally useful for acquiring details about your subject or information that wouldn't appear in a more general source. Because they tend to use the jargon and concepts associated with the discipline, they can be excellent tools for identifying terms for possible research and for helping you better understand what you read. On the downside, they can sometimes be difficult to understand if you don't already have a working knowledge of your topic.

Examples:

Historical and Cultural Dictionary of Vietnam

Encyclopedia of American Architecture

PsycINFO (database focusing on psychology and social sciences literature)

Getting Started with Books and Monographs

Books can be a great place to begin your research. As noted in the previous chapter, one big advantage of books for research is that they typically provide a wealth of information about a given topic. But what many entry-level researchers overlook is that there are many different types of books. Some or all of the following types of books might help to get you started or otherwise help to fill in gaps in your knowledge or in your research in general.

Almanac

An **almanac** is published annually and, among other things, provides lists of important dates as well as statistical information (e.g., census data). Almanacs are useful for finding specific facts, such as the birth date of a famous person, the population of a country, or the team that won the Super Bowl in 1975.

Bibliography

A bibliography is a compilation of sources and typically covers a specific topic, author, or publisher. Because they provide a list of possible source material, bibliographies can be very useful for getting started as well as for providing a focus for your research.

Dictionary

Because a **dictionary** defines words, terms, and concepts and how they're used, dictionaries can help when you encounter a word you don't know or understand. Subject dictionaries provide discipline-specific definitions and interpretations for common terms. For example, a general dictionary might define *teenager* as a person between thirteen and nineteen years of age, whereas a psychology dictionary might define *adolescent* as an individual in the process of developing from a child into an adult.

Encyclopedia

An **encyclopedia** is generally designed to provide informative overviews of a topic. For this reason, general encyclopedias are particularly good places to start when you don't know much about your topic. Subject encyclopedias are particularly useful for generating names, dates, and other information you can use to construct more effective search strategies.

Index

An index directs you to sources of information. Indexes tell you where to find material and can be arranged by any of a number of criteria, including page number, subject, author, and publication. Although some are now electronic, many valuable indexes are still produced in printed format. They may be general or specific to a particular topic or content area (e.g., short stories, historical documents, songs).

Monograph

A **monograph** is a book or report published a single time. Monographs focus on a single topic (or group of topics) or person. Because they present or discuss existing information in a very specific way, they can serve as an excellent foundation for subsequent research. A study of Picasso's use of the color blue in his paintings, for example, could be a monograph.

Before You Search for Articles

Electronic forms of information—especially articles—present some unique and distinct challenges to researchers. Lacking familiarity with the technologies, many beginning researchers become confused about what search tool to use or how to use it effectively. The next chapter offers some suggestions about how to generate successful searches.

For a number of reasons, however, even if you know which search tool to use and how to conduct a successful search, accessing and acquiring electronic articles can still be a significant source of confusion and frustration for many. A few of the main culprits are outlined in the following sections. Being aware of these considerations from the start will help you to conduct better searches and likely improve your overall research experience.

Internet versus Search Tool

Because you typically use an Internet browser to access electronic databases, indexes, and other search tools, it is easy to become confused and think you are searching the Internet. However, when you use a library search tool to look for information, you are searching a specific set of content. For example, you are *not* searching the Internet when you are searching a database such as Academic Search Complete. You are searching the content indexed by that search tool.

Browser versus Search Tool Options

Because library search tools are typically accessed via an Internet browser, it is common to use the browser buttons to navigate through your searches. For example, after viewing a citation, you are likely to click on the Back button to return to the previous screen. However, this action can cause a number of problems and should be avoided at all costs. Sometimes the problem will be obvious; other times, it won't be obvious at all. Either way, when using a library search tool, it is advisable to use the resource's buttons and features rather than your browser's. If you find you have used one of your browser's buttons or experience an otherwise inexplicable problem, the only way to address it is simply to start over.

Web-Based Periodical versus Full-Text via an Index

A growing number of printed magazines and journals now have an electronic version available via the Web. These true, online versions generally offer the full content of the periodical. Moreover, hyperlinks enable you to navigate through the item much as you would the printed version. As noted earlier, though, a key drawback is that many periodicals do not have a web-based version. Even for those that do, you may need to pay to gain access. Conversely, what's freely available may be dated or abridged.

Library indexes and databases, on the other hand, are (usually) provided free of charge to students. They also have the advantage of allowing you to search multiple periodicals simultaneously. That such search tools focus almost exclusively on content, however, is a mixed blessing. True, you do not have to sift through advertisements and other distractions. However, nonarticle content, such as job postings and conference announcements, is typically not available. Likewise, you cannot easily browse from article to article as you can on the Web. You can see and access only the articles and citations that show up in your search results.

Article Services

Confounding things further are so-called article services. Essentially, these are online companies and services that provide access to articles and periodicals. Unfortunately, the content that is available for free is often only an excerpt from an article and is often outdated. Getting the current content in its entirety typically requires some sort of fee or subscription. Even so, much of the content is from magazines, not from the professional, scholarly sorts of publications you should be using to complete your coursework. In short, though there are some decent article services out there, be careful. Before using any, speak with a librarian about availability through your library.

Getting Started with Articles

Simply going to the library and browsing periodicals to find articles on your topic is ineffective at best. Today's academic library provides access to dozens, often hundreds, of electronic indexes and other search tools that can be used to find articles, book reviews, and all sorts of other information. As with books and other resources, some are general and some are geared toward content from a specific field or discipline. Some provide direct access to the information; others require you to link to another resource, access it physically, or acquire it from another location. Because of these and other considerations, knowing which search tools to select and how to use them effectively can be confusing and, at times, a bit overwhelming. To help you past that hurdle, consider the following when selecting a search tool to locate and retrieve articles.

Content

First and foremost, you need to select the resource(s) most closely aligned with your topic. At the same time, recognize there may be other, related resources that meet your needs. A history resource and, more broadly, a humanities resource, for example, are both likely to produce information on historically significant topics and events. Consider using both.

Focus

As with content, you need to choose the resource(s) with the perspective most relevant to the one you are taking on your topic. For example, if your topic concerns nursing education, decide whether you're focusing on the nursing or the education part and choose either nursing or education resources accordingly.

Format

Because many resources index items in different formats (e.g., books, articles, documents), you need to be sure the resource you select indexes items in the format you're seeking.

Level

Not all resources index peer-reviewed or even scholarly content. Conversely, some resources provide indexing *only* for content from academic and peer-reviewed sources. Be sure the resource you are using indexes level-appropriate content.

Magazine or Journal?

Journals and magazines are published for different reasons for different audiences. Many instructors won't allow you to use information from magazine articles or, if so, only on a limited scale. The latter are geared toward leisure reading and generally do not include research or academic types of articles. Instead, you'll likely be required to use articles from scholarly or peer-reviewed journals (see chapters 4 and 10). However, unless you're familiar with a particular periodical, it's not always easy to tell a journal from a magazine, especially those in electronic format. It can be even more difficult to distinguish a scholarly journal from a peer-reviewed one.

Figure 7.2 identifies some of the elements that you can use to distinguish one type of periodical from another.

FIGURE 7.2

Differences among Types of Periodicals

	Journal	Magazine	Magazine
	Scholarly, Academic, or Peer-Reviewed	*General Interest*	*Popular*
Examples	JAMA Journal of Education	Newsweek New Yorker	People Reader's Digest
Purpose	To report on original research in order to make the information available to the academic world	To provide information in a general way to a broad audience of interested people	Entertain; sell products; promote a viewpoint; describe current events or popular culture
Appearance	Typically sober, serious look	May be attractive although some are in newspaper format	Typically very attractive
Article Author	A scholar in the discipline, someone who has conducted research, or someone with extensive experience with the topic	A member of the editorial staff or a staff writer	Staff member or freelance writer

Continued on next page

	Journal	Magazine	Magazine
	Scholarly, Academic, or Peer-Reviewed	*General Interest*	*Popular*
Language	Discipline-specific and assumes readers have some knowledge of such; statistical information often included as well	Geared to educated audience; no background is required but some material may be difficult for some to comprehend	Usually short sentences and simple language to meet minimum educational level
Depth	Lots	Some to lots	Little to none
Images	Relate to content; often include charts and graphs; few glossy or "interesting" pictures	Often heavily illustrated or contains photographs	Lots of photos, drawings, and other colorful, glossy graphics
Advertisements	If any, pertain to content or focus of publication	Frequent and consumer-oriented; may (or may not) have something to do with content of publication	Frequent and consumer-oriented
Citations	Sources *always* cited; documentation often extensive	Some cite sources; some do not	Sources rarely, if ever, cited; information often acquired through secondary sources
Publisher	Most often a professional organization, university, or academic press	Usually published by a commercial entity; some published by professional organizations	Published solely by commercial entities or individuals
Review	Articles subject to review by board or others with experience or background in the subject	Editors may or may not have expertise in discipline	Editors review for commercial value

Getting Started with Websites

Even though you may not have found what you wanted, if you are in college, it is almost a given that you have searched the Internet for information at some point. Most of us have one search engine we use more than others. In the past, Lycos and AltaVista were the search engines of choice. Today, though, they have all but been forgotten with the advent of Google. The intent here is not to promote one search engine over another, but because it is familiar to so many, Google will serve as our example.

Advanced Search Options

When most people do a search of the Internet, they use the basic, default search options provided by the search engine, often just a **keyword search**. To increase your success, however, strive to use search engines that have advanced search options. For example, limiting your search to sites that include your keywords in a specific location within the site, such as the site's URL, and eliminating sites in a language you do not speak are common options.

Google Scholar (http://scholar.google.com)

Again, the intent here is not to promote one search engine over another. But, when searching for the more scholarly, more academic sorts of information on the Internet, you will be well served to try **Google Scholar** as a starting point. From Google Scholar's own About page:

> Google Scholar provides a simple way to broadly search for scholarly literature. From one place, you can search across many disciplines and sources: articles, theses, books, abstracts and court opinions, from academic publishers, professional societies, online repositories, universities and other web sites. Google Scholar helps you find relevant work across the world of scholarly research. (http://scholar.google.com/intl/en/scholar/about.html)

This does not guarantee that you will find relevant material or that your results sets will necessarily be smaller. But it at least eliminates a lot of non-academic sites from your searches.

Interlibrary Loan (ILL)

It is impossible for a library to have or even provide access to every piece of information ever produced. However, for a number of reasons, you should never eliminate a source from your list of potential resources simply because your library does not provide access to it. For example, acquiring that article or book may save you hours of additional research or otherwise facilitate your work. For books and articles, academic libraries participate in various agreements with one another through which they share resources. This service is typically referred to as interlibrary loan, or ILL.

To request an item via ILL, you typically submit a brief form with your contact information as well as the citation information for the item you are seeking. In most cases, libraries offer this service free of charge or for a nominal fee. Because they are usually sent electronically, articles often arrive in just one to two days; because they are often sent through the postal service, books may take a little longer. Despite the speed of such services, when requesting an item from another library, budget enough time to get the item, read it, and take notes from it.

❓ REFLECTIONS

- Speak with a librarian about how to acquire information sources not directly available at your library. Identify time and cost factors, if any.
- Identify one general index and one subject-specific index related to your topic or discipline.
- Select an index from two different vendors (e.g., EBSCO, ProQuest) and note similarities and differences between the two. Ask a librarian for assistance if you're having trouble locating resources from two different vendors.
- Locate at least one subject-specific dictionary or subject-specific encyclopedia for your major course of study. If there is not an exact match, find one that is close and browse through the index and table of contents for specific references to your discipline.
- Select a popular or general interest magazine and compare it to a scholarly or academic journal. What similarities and differences do you see?
- Examine an article from each of the preceding sources. What similarities and differences do you see?

CHAPTER 8

Constructing Effective Search Strategies

. . . .

T he list of information search tools from which to choose is ever increasing. Because of individual differences among search tools, though, there is substantial variability in terms of how one resource looks compared to another. As a result, generating and conducting effective searches can be extremely challenging, to say the least. Even for experienced researchers, generating successful searches can sometimes be extremely cumbersome and intimidating. Still, despite their differences, most search tools have a variety of common features and functions. This chapter focuses on strategies and concepts you can apply to virtually any search tool.

It is important to note that there are still some printed resources that can be used to track down sources of information. However, if you are a first-time researcher, it is highly unlikely that they will play more than a minor role in your research. The overwhelming majority of search tools you are likely to encounter and use will be electronic in nature. For this reason, the concepts, strategies, and tips in this chapter focus almost exclusively on electronic resources. Be aware, though, that many of the basic concepts will apply to their printed counterparts.

Interface Challenges
. . . .

A search tool's interface is one of the key obstacles students face when starting their research. The term *interface* refers to how a search tool looks. It is essentially the graphic representation of the features within the search tool. Unfortunately, because different search tools are produced by different vendors, there are as many interfaces as there are vendors. Interfaces also change regularly—often without notice. Features of an interface may have been moved or changed or even taken away entirely since the last time you used it. Also, new features and search options may have been added.

Most students understand this on some level. So, what's the problem? Arguably, the biggest problem with interfaces is the lack of consistent functionality. That is, a search that works in one search tool may or may not work in another. Field searching is a good example (and will be explained in more detail later in this chapter).

Let's say you want to find books by Shakespeare. The following shows how you might perform this search using two different tools.

Tool 1: Author = Shakespeare

Tool 2: AU "Shakespeare"

Both tools will generate a list of works by authors named Shakespeare. But, as you can see, how you conduct the search is different for each resource. As a result, entering AU "Shakespeare" in search tool 1, for example, is likely to generate few, if any, results—even though there are likely to be books by that author. This is because that search is not formatted properly, in the way recognized by the search tool. The presence (or lack) of elements such as quotation marks ("") or parentheses [( )] can change the results you get, even within the same tool!

Do *Not* Give Up!

Don't despair! Despite the wide variety of interfaces, all hope is not lost. As noted earlier, there are many common concepts and strategies you can use for most search tools. The rest of this chapter focuses on some of the more common ideas and techniques you are likely to employ.

Keyword versus Field Searching

When using a search tool to find information, you will be doing two types of searching. Neither is better than the other. In fact, there may be times when combining both types of searches into a single search will produce the results you're seeking. Either way, you need to understand the role and relative strengths and weaknesses of each in order to determine which is the most appropriate search for you.

Keyword Searching

A keyword search is the broadest of all possible searches and can be used to search for books, articles, or websites. It is the default search mechanism for most search tools. With a basic keyword search, the search tool produces results based on matching text. Where it looks and how it retrieves hits vary by resource. For example, the keyword you search for could be in the item's title or the abstract. Too, the words may appear side by side or not. Because the search tool is simply matching the text you've entered, you are as likely to find articles on *wolf* (animal) as by *wolf* (author's name) or about *wolf* (the big bad wolf).

- Advantages:
  - ‣ Can broaden your search easily and quickly
  - ‣ Is the default search for most information resources
  - ‣ Is good for browsing for concepts and possible search terms
  - ‣ Can search multiple resources similarly
- Disadvantage:
  - ‣ Is likely to produce a significant number of irrelevant results

Field Searching

With a **field search**, you are conducting a keyword search for matching text in a specific field within a search tool. As a result, field searching can be a quick and easy way to focus your results. Available fields vary from resource to resource. Too, there may be variations in how they are displayed or accessed. But the functionality of field searching remains consistent across resources. That is, an author search in any resource will search for matches in the author field of the search tool.

Using the earlier example, say you remember reading a book last year but can remember only that the author's name was *Wolf*. If you simply did a keyword search for *wolf*, your results would likely include references to the animal *wolf* as well as to works for which *Wolf* is listed as the author. Conducting an author search would focus your results on works authored by *Wolf*.

- Advantage:
  - ‣ Can focus your searching quickly and easily
- Disadvantages:
  - ‣ Words must generally match those in the field *exactly* or no matches will be found
  - ‣ Because field names and how you search them differ from search tool to search tool, effective multiple, simultaneous resource searching is virtually impossible

☑ TIPS

- Start with broad, keyword searches.
- When possible, mix and match keyword and field searches to find as many resources as possible and to generate additional search terms.
- Remember that even though fields may have different names in different resources, they function the same way. For example, one resource may use the term *subject* while another uses *descriptor*. Both, though, refer to the subject of the record.
- Try entering alternate terms or variant spellings (e.g., teenager, adolescent, minor).
- Examine a relevant record to see what terms are being used and then conduct a field search using the search tool's terms.

Two of the more common field searches you are likely to conduct are author and subject.

Author Searching

As discussed in our earlier example, an author search searches the records' author field for the name you've entered. For example, an author search for *Shakespeare* would produce all records with *Shakespeare* in the author field. Similarly, say you find an article by *Grayson* that is really useful. You could focus your search on other books and articles authored by *Grayson*. Most resources use the format *last name, first initial/name* to search. For *Shakespeare*, you could try one of the following three searches:

Shakespeare

Shakespeare, W

Shakespeare, William

✔ TIPS

- Because most academic authors tend to write about the same subject matter, clicking on the author's name may produce additional information on your topic by that author.
- For author searches, use the last name. If that's too broad (e.g., Smith), try adding a first initial, separated from the last name by a comma (e.g., Smith, A).
- Because first names of authors may often be entered in a number of ways, if use of the whole name doesn't work, try just the first initial. For example, *William* could be *W, Wm, Will, Bill,* or even *Guillaume.*

Subject Searching

A subject search is a specific type of field searching that allows you to focus a search on a specific topic or subject by searching only the subject field within a search tool's records. The tricky part is finding the right term or terms to enter. Starting with a keyword search is helpful. For example, you might enter *World War One* as a subject search. This is perfectly reasonable. If few or no results are produced, that doesn't necessarily mean there is no information on your topic. It means there are simply no records matching your criteria. Trying *First World War* or *World War I* might be more effective. From there, look at the search tool's subject field to see what terms are being used and use them to generate a subject search.

When individuals input data into an index, they use what is called a **controlled vocabulary** to standardize the words they use. Because multiple people are likely to be working on the index, a controlled vocabulary ensures that similar information is indexed in the same way. In this case, the proper subject term might be *world war 1914-1918.* If so, the search for *World War One* would not produce any results because *one* does not appear in the subject field (i.e., it is not the controlled vocabulary term being used in this resource).

The **Library of Congress Subject Headings (LCSH)** are a commonly used controlled vocabulary of subject terms used by many librarians to organize items within their collections. Among other things, LCSH can be used as a thesaurus of sorts for identifying possible subject terms as well as broader, narrower, and related terms. The Library of Congress's website provides an outline of LCSH (www.loc.gov/aba/cataloging/subject/).

☑ TIPS

- When you find a relevant source…

  ▸ Click on the appropriate subject heading or headings within the search tool to generate a list of other items on the same subject.

  ▸ Write down other subject headings that might be useful for subsequent searches.

- If you're having difficulty identifying the correct subject heading to use, use the same term or terms to conduct a keyword search and look at the subject field of relevant sources.

- Because controlled vocabularies often vary by resource (particularly those produced by different vendors), be aware that a subject search that works in one resource may not work in another.

- Because academic libraries shelve books by subject, find the appropriate area for your topic and browse until you find a book you like. Then, locate that book in the library's catalog, determine the controlled vocabulary for the book, and click on the appropriate subject link(s) to find related books on your topic.

Strategies for Improving Your Searches

Because everyone's topic and information needs vary, it is impossible to discuss every possible effective search strategy. Moreover, because of differences between interfaces and other factors, no single search strategy will work in every resource every time. As you become more familiar with the research process, you are likely to develop a personal style that you find to be most successful. There are some universal things you can do to improve your searching effectiveness—regardless of which search tool you are using. As you read through the rest of this chapter, you might also want to refer to chapter 13—it provides a working example of an actual search employing some of the strategies outlined here. Figure 8.1 summarizes some of the general strategies you can employ to narrow or broaden your search.

FIGURE 8.1

Search Strategies to Narrow or Broaden Results

Strategy	To Narrow Results	To Broaden Results
Different Terms	Use the controlled vocabulary of the resource Select words from the various fields within a relevant record Search for phrases and compound terms	Try a keyword search Use synonyms Try alternate spellings Identify variables that might impact your terms
Different Perspective	Focus on one perspective	Look at your topic from more than one perspective
Different Strategy	Try a subject (or other field) search Impose one or more limits Combine searches Combine strategies	Try a keyword search Remove search limit(s) Check your spelling Check your typing
Different Syntax	Use ALL or AND searching	Use OR searching
Different Resource	Use a subject-specific resource	Try a general interest resource

Strategy 1: Be Patient with Yourself and the Process

First and foremost, it is important to always keep in mind that research is a process (see figure 1.2, p. 7). It is inevitable that you will encounter challenges and frustrations along the way. Among these is the fact that it is highly unlikely that trying one search in one resource will produce exactly the information you need to complete your assignment. To be effective, you will need to combine a variety of strategies and techniques. Doing so will take time and effort. It will also require patience and persistence. Rest assured, though, as with most things in life, the more you do research, the easier it will become.

Strategy 2: Check Your Spelling and Your Typing

If you misspell or mistype a word—or, worse, misspell *and* mistype a word—you are likely to generate little, if any, information on your topic. *Always* check your spelling and your typing for accuracy, particularly if you are getting limited results in your initial searches.

Strategy 3: Try Different Search Terms and Keywords

No matter which search tool you use, you need to submit at least one search term for the tool to be able to retrieve information. The problem often lies in determining which is the best term to use. Most researchers start with a few key concepts and terms. Then, as they begin their research, they encounter others that they use to conduct additional searches. If you are having difficulty generating appropriate search terms on your own, try one or more of the following tips to generate a running list of possible concepts, names, and other terms related to your topic that you might use to conduct your research.

Start with What You Know

As you consider what term or terms to use to conduct your search for information, reflect on what you already know about the topic. You don't have to be an expert to know something about your topic. Even if you don't know much about your topic, consider your feelings and experiences. For example, are you for or against the topic? What about the topic caused you to choose it for a research assignment? Do you know someone who has had a similar experience or who has talked about your topic? Write these thoughts and feelings down and try to generate some initial keywords you can use to conduct a search.

Browse Source Material

Browse through some articles, books, and other resources. This is a particularly useful strategy if you do not know a whole lot about your topic. Some libraries provide resources geared specifically toward entry-level researchers. These resources often provide background, chronologies, pros and cons, and other useful information about a variety of topics and are a great tool for developing a list of possible search terms. Reference works such as encyclopedias and almanacs can also be helpful for generating some initial search terms.

Examine Your Purpose Statement for Impact Words

When developing a list of possible search terms, you should always examine your purpose statement. To do this, first, write down your purpose statement. Next, separate the *noise words* from your *impact words*. Your impact words can serve as a starting point. Here is a sample research topic:

> The effect of classroom technology on the academic achievement of high school students.

IMPACT WORDS

> *classroom technology, academic achievement, high school (students)*

Impact words are those words that carry meaning. They outline the focus of your research. For words such as *students*, you need to decide how to use them. Here, you could search the word *students* independently (broader) or as attached at the end of *high school* (narrower).

NOISE WORDS

> *the, effect, of, on*

Noise words are words that are redundant, don't add meaning, or don't carry any content value. Unless such words are part of an exact phrase (e.g., "*A* tale *of* two cities"), they can and should generally be ignored and not incorporated into your search strategy. In the example, *effect* is also a noise word because it is redundant. Your research will result in an understanding of the effect of classroom technology. You don't need to conduct a specific search for *effect*. That said, adding a modifying term such as *psychological* would cause *effect* to evolve into an impact word because you're hoping to uncover information about a particular type of effect.

Develop a List of Related and Alternate Terms

How many ways can you say the same thing? Very rarely will a single term or set of search terms produce all the information you want and need. You may have to do several related searches to find the information you're seeking. For example, although the terms *adolescents* and *teenagers* refer to the same group of individuals, a search on each will produce somewhat different results. The two sets of results will likely have some overlap, but they are not likely to be the same because you are searching for two different terms, and, therefore, you will generate two different sets of results. To conduct the best, most exhaustive search possible, you should search both terms as well as any others you can think of that describe the same thing.

Although it's true that some terms just don't have synonyms, many do. Once you've developed your initial set of terms, go through the list and try to come up with at least one alternate term or concept for each term on your initial list of impact words. In this case, you might also try words like *minors*, *young adults*, *teens*, or *teen agers* (two words rather than just one).

> *classroom technology*: instructional technology, teaching technology, educational technology, computer-assisted instruction

> *academic achievement*: scholastic achievement, academic performance, scholastic performance, grades

> *high school students*: secondary school students

Identify Alternate Spellings

Every once in a while, a search is rendered ineffective because of the use of an incorrect or uncommon spelling. This doesn't mean you've spelled the term incorrectly. It just means the spelling isn't recognized by the search tool. When alternate spellings exist, try them all. The same is true for abbreviations. If an abbreviation doesn't work, try spelling out the entire term, and vice versa. The following are some examples:

Brazil	←→	Brasil
Symphony	←→	Symphonie
Gray	←→	Grey
9	←→	IX
VW	←→	Volkswagen

Identify Broader and Narrower Terms

Sometimes you have to be a little creative. If you're finding too many records, you'll need to narrow your focus. Conversely, if you're not finding enough, you may need to broaden your search parameters. One way of doing so is to search for terms that are broader or narrower than the ones you are using. The following *italicized* words give you a sense of some broader (more general) and narrower (more specific) terms you might try for the earlier example.

classroom technology

> Narrower: A specific type of classroom technology, such as *smart boards* or *calculators*

> Broader: Classroom technology is a subset of *computers* or *technology*

academic achievement

> Narrower: Academic achievement as measured by a specific type of test, such as the *Scholastic Achievement Test* or *SAT*

> Broader: Academic achievement is a topic associated with the broader topics of *academics* or *student achievement*

high school students

> Narrower: A specific grade (e.g., *ninth, 9th*) or level of high school students (e.g., *freshman*)

Broader: High school students are part of the larger category called *students*

✅ TIPS

- As you read, watch for new words, different ways of saying the same thing, or your search terms used in a different way. Many of these words can be used to generate subsequent searches for information on your topic.
- Try looking at terms and concepts from other perspectives. *Video games*, for example, could be a business topic as easily as an educational or psychological one.
- Be aware that although they provide excellent starting points, terms that work well in one search tool may not work in another.
- Examine existing sources, such as your textbook or a subject encyclopedia on your topic.
- Conduct a few preliminary searches and skim through some of the records that result. You don't necessarily have to read the whole book or article. Simply browse the table of contents, read the abstract, or examine relevant sections, jotting down keywords as you go.
- Try a number of terms and concepts. One search on one word or set of words will not find all the relevant information on your topic.

Strategy 4: Identify Possible Variables Affecting Your Terms

When searching for information, simply identifying the correct terms to use in a search tool isn't enough. An equally important part is understanding the context of your topic and the variables that might affect it. That is, certain factors may affect which terms you should use. For example, if you are doing research on the history of movies, time period is important. Although we refer to them as *movies* now, they were originally known as *moving pictures* and, later, as *motion pictures*. Some variables affecting your topic in this way include these:

Time period	Geography/location
Race	Gender
Ethnicity	Age

Strategy 5: Identify Your Perspective on Your Topic

As with the variables just noted, perspective may also impact how you search for information. For example, say you are doing a paper on teen pregnancy. You could research the topic from the point of view of teenage mothers or the doctors who work with them. You could examine possible causes or the impact of teen pregnancy on society. Knowing what aspect or perspective you want to take on your topic will help focus the terms and search tools you are likely to use.

Strategy 6: Add or Remove Search Limits (Filters)

A **limit** is a quick way to narrow your search along a common criterion. When you use **search limits**, or **filters**, all the results that emerge must match the criteria. Examples of common limits include peer-reviewed, full-text, and date range. Setting a date range of 2010 to 2015, for example, would limit your results set to information published between 2010 and 2015. Some limits, such as date range and language, are general and common to most resources. Others are specific to a particular resource or discipline. For example, a psychology database may enable you to limit your search to a particular gender or to human or nonhuman psychology.

Strategy 7: Try Multiple Search Strategies and Combine Different Techniques

This brings us full circle. Remember, research is a process. As a result, there is no single, magic method for producing good results every time in every search tool. Combine a keyword search with a subject field search. Add a limit to focus your search or remove one to broaden it. Try different terms. Search through another search tool. The best, most effective research involves a variety of techniques, terms, and strategies.

Search Syntax

Search syntax refers to the way you enter your search into a search tool. Entering the words themselves is certainly important, but how you do so is equally important, if not more so. For example, there may be times you will want to search for more than a single word at a time, or you may want to search multiple words as a phrase. How you would do so in a given resource may or may not be the same as in another. You may need to use radio buttons or drop-down menus, or you may have to type things in manually. Regardless of how it's done, there are a few core ideas you need to be aware of when constructing more sophisticated searches. Speak with a librarian to learn which of these options are available in the resource you're using and how to incorporate them into your searches.

Boolean Operators (Logical Operators)

A **Boolean operator**, or **logical operator**, is a word or symbol used to make a logical connection between two or more search terms. The two most common Boolean operators are *AND* and *OR*. They can be used to narrow or broaden your search, respectively.

Searching ALL (Boolean = AND)

Virtually every search you conduct will involve more than one word. Typically one modifies the other. For example, you might be exploring how various authors use foreboding in literature. With most resources, the default search is a keyword search that will search for all the words you've entered. If that's not the case, look for a Search ALL button or menu option. Failing that, try separating your words with AND to search for *this* AND *that*. Speak with a librarian to learn how to use AND properly in the resource you're using.

> *adolescents AND teenagers* will find all records containing both terms

Searching ANY (Boolean = OR)

Sometimes you may want to search similar, related terms simultaneously. Say you're doing a paper on police dogs. You think *dog*, *canine*, or *K-9* might be the best terms. By searching ANY, you will find records that contain at least one of the three words. In this way, you've broadened your search. If there is not a drop-down menu option or a Search ANY button, try separating your words with OR to retrieve matches that contain either *this* OR *that*. Speak with a librarian to learn how to use OR properly (e.g., it may or may not need to be capitalized) in the resource you're using.

adolescents OR teenagers will find all records containing either or both terms

Phrase Searching

Sometimes you'll want to search for words in a specific order. Compound nouns, such as *social security* and *national football league*, and book titles are good examples. Surrounding your phrase with quotation marks—for example, "social security"—or parentheses—(national football league)—are common ways of grouping terms together for **phrase searching**. Again, a librarian can assist you with the proper syntax for these types of searches.

Capital Letters

Most resources do not require or expect you to use uppercase letters when entering your search terms. *South Africa* is likely to be understood as *south africa* and vice versa.

Truncation

Truncation refers to the use of a character at the end of a string of text to find all variations of a root term. The "*" in *commun**, for example, would find not only commun*ism*, commun*al*, and commun*istic* but also commun-*ication* and commun*ity*.

Wildcard

Most information tools recognize what are called *wildcards*. As with truncation, a wildcard is a symbol that takes the place of letters in a string of text. But, instead of appearing at the end, it is placed in the middle. This is an excellent tool for words that have more than one spelling. For example, instead of doing separate searches for *Brazil* and *Brasil*, entering *Bra?il* will find both spellings.

Searching Multiple Resources Simultaneously

As you consider various search strategies, realize that a growing number of academic libraries provide **unified search tools**. These enable you to search multiple search tools simultaneously. Sometimes you can select which tools to search; other times you have to search the entire list. On the plus side, simultaneous searching is likely to produce more results and is therefore a good tool for browsing. Yet, because unified search tools typically search by keyword and because they are sifting through search tools on a variety of topics, you will likely have to go through a greater number of irrelevant results than if you'd conducted searches on the search tools individually.

If at all, it is more than likely that you will be able to limit your search to a specific search tool or group of search tools only *after* your initial search. However, if you decide to use a unified search tool *and* if you are able to choose what to search, be sure the search tools you select are reasonably related to your topic. Searching an agricultural resource, for example, will be a waste of time unless your topic has something to do with farming, animal husbandry, or related agricultural topics and concerns. For these and other reasons, you may ultimately find it more productive to search one search tool well than to search several poorly.

Search History

Many search tools provide users with a **search history**. As the name suggests, a search history literally provides a record of the terms, limits, and strategies you've used so far and the results that were generated from your searches. One big advantage of search histories is that they provide you with a way to see what's working and what's not. Most also allow you to combine and refine your searches accordingly. Being able to save your search history is also beneficial in that it saves you time later on. For example, say you spend an hour doing research. If you save your search history, you don't have to start over later and retrace your steps. You can simply access your search history and continue from where you left off.

Searching the Internet

Searching the Internet poses its own unique set of challenges. As has already been discussed, there are dozens of search engines you can use to search for information, each with its own strengths and weaknesses. Still, because they all function in a similar manner, many of the search strategies and techniques described earlier apply to searching the Internet as well.

Two notable exceptions, though, are the lack of a controlled vocabulary and the inability to conduct specific field searches. Among other things, this means it is impossible to conduct a specific search for websites on a particular subject or author as outlined earlier. The best you can do is to match keywords. That's why a search for *china* is as likely to generate results on the country as it is on the style of dinnerware.

That said, this doesn't mean there aren't ways of focusing your search of the Internet. Two suggestions are summarized next.

Learn How the Search Engine You Use Works

A search engine is essentially a piece of software that locates and retrieves web pages, files, and other documents. The metaphor of a spider and its web is often used to describe how search engines work. If you think of the terms you're using as the "fly"—the information you want to find on the Internet—the "spider" or search engine is what finds and retrieves the information from the Web.

That said, how each search engine searches the Web for the words you've submitted and how the results are ranked are typically company secrets. This means you may or may not be able to determine the details about how it functions. However, most search engines use some sort of location and frequency data. That is, results are generated and ranked based on how often your word appears and where on a site. For example, sites on which your keyword appears more often than on others or sites on which the word appears in the site's title suggest a higher level of relevancy and, therefore, are likely to appear higher on your list of results. Looking at a search engine's Help option can assist you in better understanding how your search engine works.

Use the Advanced Search Option

The default search for most search engines is a basic keyword search. However, a search engine's advanced search option usually provides a number of additional ways to limit your searches. For example, you can select where you want to search for the words you have chosen. Title, URL, and the content part of a website are common. Other limits allow you to focus your search on sites written in a language you can read and on specific document types, such as PDF.

- Familiarize yourself with more than one search engine. Because each search engine searches the Internet differently, it is likely to have different search features, which, in turn, may generate sites that other search engines do not.
- Select a subject-specific search engine (if available). For example, if you're seeking government information, try a search engine that searches only the .gov domain.
- Try strategies using the techniques and methods discussed earlier for indexes.

Locating Nontextual Information

There may be times you will want (or be expected) to incorporate non-textual material into your paper, such as a photo, chart, or picture. You might also want to find a media file as part of a presentation of your findings. These nontextual resources can be great sources of information and should not be overlooked as part of your research strategy. Realize, though, that use of the image or video might involve considerable editing on your part in order to be able to incorporate it into your paper or presentation. For example, perhaps you want to include a photograph of someone closely aligned with your topic. If you can't locate it directly, you need to either decide a photo isn't needed or look for some other image you can use.

Unfortunately, finding the exact image or clip you want may take considerable time and effort. Most resources you'll use to find books and articles have very little search capability in this respect. At best, you might be able to limit your search to items that have images. However, it is highly unlikely you'll be able to limit the search to the specific image (e.g., the president saluting the troops) or type of image (e.g., a bar chart) that you're seeking.

 TIPS

- Only use images that contribute to the understanding of your topic or the point you're trying to make.
- For books, look for a list of illustrations or photographs. Often pictures can be found in a separate section near the center of the book.

- Do not use images as space fillers.
- To find nontextual information, you're likely to have greater success using the image search feature of whatever search engine you use to search the Internet.
- As with text, be sure to properly cite the source from which you retrieve the image.

Revising Your Topic

Students change their topics all the time and for any number of reasons. Sometimes the reasons are appropriate. For example, as you learn more about your topic, you might learn something new and want to focus your research on that particular aspect. Many times, though, students want to change their topic for inappropriate reasons, such as being unable to find enough information. If you're having problems in this respect, review chapter 5 about choosing a topic. Likewise, try the tips and strategies summarized in this chapter or speak with a librarian to learn how to search more effectively. Either way, before you change your topic, be sure to speak with your instructor to learn the consequences of doing so.

❓ REFLECTIONS

- Using your thesis statement, develop a list of at least five keywords you might use to begin your search.
    - Identify one broader and one narrower term or concept.
    - Select any two and combine them into a single search using AND. Then, use the same two words but combine them using OR and note the differences and similarities between the two searches.
- Use the preceding keywords to conduct a preliminary search in a search tool of your choosing. Select one thread that looks interesting and examine the subject field. Identify at least one subject term used by the index that you might use to focus or refine your search.
- Select a limit (e.g., full-text, date range) to focus your search even further.

- Click on the author's name of one of the articles you think might be relevant. Did you find other articles by the same author that might be useful in your research?

- Select two similar or related keywords from the list you just developed to conduct a search of the Internet. For example, select *women* and *females*. Compare and contrast the results of each search. What is the same and what is different, especially in terms of (a) the number of results and (b) the type of information conveyed in the results?

- Conduct a search for articles on a compound term (e.g., social security, old age, elementary school) using your search tool's options. Then, conduct the same search using quotation marks or parentheses around the terms. Compare and contrast both types of search. Which one seemed to produce more of the types of results you were expecting?

CHAPTER 9

Understanding Search Results

. . . .

Before you begin evaluating the sources you find to determine if they're useful to you, you need to understand the results generated from your searches. All too often, first-time researchers overlook obvious resources and get upset because they're not finding what they want. Others have difficulty simply accessing the item(s) they've found. Having a better understanding of results sets can help you conduct more effective searches in the future.

"Garbage In, Garbage Out"
. . . .

When searching for information, it is important to keep this phrase in mind. That is, when attempting to understand why your search didn't produce the results you expected, you need to remember that a search will retrieve only items that match your search criteria. Translation? Your results will be only as good as your search strategy and will reflect only the search you conducted. If you conduct a weak or incorrect search (i.e., garbage in), your results are likely to be disappointing as well (i.e., garbage out).

 TIPS ————————————————————————

- There is no perfect number of results, but, as a rule of thumb, if you retrieve one hundred or fewer records, you've done a pretty focused search; more than one hundred records is good for browsing and brainstorming.

MYTHS ABOUT RESULTS LISTS

When talking about lists of results, a few key myths need to be dispelled.

Myth of Relevancy

One of the biggest obstacles to overcome is the idea that if an item is retrieved, it's relevant and appropriate to your needs. This is typically more of a problem with keyword searching than with other types because of the larger quantity of results that are generated. But even field and other types of searching can return sources that aren't what you're seeking.

Myth of Scarcity

This is the opposite of the myth of relevancy. Here, just because few or no results come back doesn't mean there isn't any information available on your topic. Although there may be times when this is true, typically small results sets mean one of three things: (1) you've done a very effective search, (2) you've conducted a very ineffective search, or (3) there simply isn't a lot of information on your topic.

Myth of Immediacy

Because full-text items are readily available and very convenient, many researchers limit their results to full-text. However, just because something isn't available in full-text doesn't mean it's not available. Usually it's simply not available in the resource you're searching. The item may be available via another resource, in the library, or via another library. Limiting your search to full-text only may unnecessarily eliminate a vast number of other resources on your topic.

Myth of Existence

Just because you think there should be a book or an article on a topic doesn't mean that there is. There may, however, be related resources. For example, there may not be a specific book on the oil industry in Oil City, Pennsylvania. There may, however, be a book on the oil industry in Pennsylvania or on the petroleum industry in general that may have information on your topic.

- Generally speaking, small results sets mean either you're doing a very effective search, not many items match your criteria, or you're doing something incorrectly.
- Ask a librarian about interlibrary loan services to acquire books, articles, and other items your library doesn't have.

Locating Materials

Now that you've developed a list of potentially useful sources, how do you go about retrieving them? As noted earlier, there are three general locations for information: physically in the library, electronically, and on the Web. More and more items are available electronically directly from various search tools. A growing number of items are also available on the Web. But, there is still a vast amount of information that is available only in a physical format, such as print or microform. These items are accessible only in the library.

In addition, keep in mind that no library can possibly provide access to every published piece of information. This doesn't mean you should discard a source of information just because you cannot directly acquire a copy of it. Many items not available directly from your library, especially books and articles, can be requested by your librarian through interlibrary loan (ILL) from other libraries.

Locating Books and Monographs

Libraries typically shelve their books by subject. Books also tend to be shelved from the general to the more specific. For example, all the books on eating disorders will generally be shelved in the same area. Within that section, there will be subsections containing books on specific types of eating disorders, such as bulimia. Larger institutions may have more than one library so you may have to visit multiple libraries to acquire the books you want.

Monographs may also be shelved by subject, often alongside books on the same subject. However, many libraries shelve monographs by collection. For example, a library might house its collection of government documents separately from other materials. Such collections may be shelved by subject or by some other criterion (e.g., the department or agency that produced the document).

Call Numbers

Librarians use what are called *call numbers* to differentiate between subjects and subclasses within subjects. The call number for a book is typically found on a small label on the spine or cover. Two primary classification schemes are used to assign call numbers—the Dewey Decimal Classification system and the Library of Congress Classification scheme.

DEWEY DECIMAL CLASSIFICATION SYSTEM

The Dewey Decimal Classification system uses a series of numbers to designate topical areas. For example, the call numbers for general books on natural sciences and mathematics start with 500. Within that broad category, books on physics begin with 530. Within the 530s, call numbers for books on heat start with 536 and those on magnetism with 538. Letters and numbers to the right of the decimal point reflect even more specificity within a subclass, such as convection for heat.

The Dewey system is used primarily by public schools. Most academic libraries don't use it. Still, you might see it used to organize collections of materials most likely to be used by those involved with public schools, such as juvenile books and curriculum kits.

LIBRARY OF CONGRESS CLASSIFICATION SCHEME

Most academic libraries use the Library of Congress (LC) Classification scheme. The LC scheme uses a unique series of letters and numbers to identify subject areas. For example, call numbers for items on science in general begin with Q while books on physics begin with QC. Following the letters, numbers distinguish one aspect of physics from another. For example, books on heat will be found within the range QC251–338.5 while books on magnetism will be found in the range QC750–766.

If you are looking for a general, introductory text that explains basic concepts and ideas in physics, Isaac Asimov's *Understanding Physics* may appear in your list of results. In Dewey, the book's call number is 530.A83 while in LC, the same book's call number is QC23.A8. Because call numbers progress alphabetically and numerically in sequential order, to locate this book, you will need to find the respective section (500s or QCs) and progress through until you find the book.

- In addition to the call number, pay attention to the floor, collection, and library in which the item is stored.
- For some e-books, you may need to install a proprietary viewer or other software to access and navigate the book.

Locating Articles

The process for locating articles is generally more straightforward than it is for books. That's because a growing number of resources provide direct access to articles. Even if it's not available directly in the resource you're searching, linking technology is being used by a growing number of libraries. This technology links you to other resources providing the full-text of the article you're seeking. In many cases, it will also tell you whether a printed version is available in your library.

Shelving of Printed Periodicals

Every library shelves periodicals differently. When looking for the printed version of a journal, consider the following:

- Journals may be shelved alphabetically or by call number (along with books), usually in sequential order (by date or volume).
- Many journals are shelved according to an acronym or abbreviation (e.g., the *Journal of the American Medical Association* might be shelved under *JAMA*).
- Journals may be available in print or on microform (especially older volumes) or both.
- Current journals may or may not be shelved alongside older issues.
- To help preserve them, older issues are often given a hard cover and called *bound journals*. Many times, bound journals have a unique location within a library.

Locating E-versions of Articles

Many students search for articles using the Internet. In many cases, this will lead you to a vendor's site (e.g., EBSCO, ProQuest). The bad news is that many of these sites require you to have an account to access the article. The good news is that many of these articles may be available through your library (rather than directly from the vendor) in either printed or electronic form. When you encounter this situation, speak with a librarian to determine the article's availability.

Understanding Web Results

Understanding a list of results from a web search can be challenging. First of all, most searches return tens of thousands of possible sites. Moreover, different search engines typically produce different sets of results using the exact same search strategy. In addition, you can't search the Internet by subject. Finally, the fact that most results lists now include advertisements, sponsored sites and links, and other extras only compounds the confusion. Understanding how sites are arranged can help to reduce or eliminate a lot of this confusion.

As outlined in chapter 8, when you type a word into a search engine, it retrieves sites that include that word. But how a search engine assigns weight to the matches found in a search is different for every search engine. Some rank results by how often the search words appear. Others focus on location. Most use a combination of the two. Generally speaking, the more criteria a term meets, the higher the site will appear on your list of results. For example, a site on which your term appears only once is likely to appear lower in the results list than sites on which the word appears multiple times. This doesn't make that site any more or any less relevant. It just helps you to understand why the site appears where it does in your list of results. Some of the ranking criteria used by search engines include the following:

- The number of times that the search words appear on a site
- How close to the top of a page the search terms appear
- Whether or not the terms appear in the page's URL, title, subheadings, links, or meta-tags
- The number of other pages that link to a particular site
- How long a page has existed

Finally, be aware that groups and individuals can pay to increase their visibility on lists of search results.

❓ REFLECTIONS

- Speak with a librarian to learn what, if any, special areas are used in your library to house unique collections (e.g., oversized books, government documents, law collections).

- Identify the library on your campus most closely aligned with your major and courses.

- Use two different search engines to conduct the same search. Then, compare results to see what's different and what's the same.

- Identify the section in your library where books on your topic are most likely to be shelved. What is the call number range associated with these books?

- How and by what criteria does your library shelve its periodicals?

- Learn more about how search engines rank results by examining sites such as searchenginewatch.com. Then, conduct exactly the same search for information on two different search engines and find a site that appears on both lists of results. Try to identify what factors may have influenced why the site appears higher on one list than on the other.

CHAPTER 10

Reading and Evaluating Information

. . . .

Reading for research is significantly different from leisure reading. When you read for research purposes, you need to read critically, making judgments about both relevancy and accuracy. This means being able to read and understand the content as well as to recognize main ideas and key concepts. It also means being able to recognize interrelationships between your readings and then being able to combine these ideas into new concepts or ideas of your own. The quality of your final paper depends on the degree to which you critically read and understand information and find the most relevant and accurate sources.

Common Reading Challenges
. . . .

Because it is a different type of reading, even those who love to read often struggle with reading for research. Review chapter 2 for additional tips and strategies for reading more efficiently and more effectively. The following are some specific reading challenges you are likely to encounter:

1. *Reading too slowly*: Reading more quickly won't improve comprehension. However, reading slowly doesn't necessarily help either. You need to find a pace that works for you and that will enable you to complete your assignment by the date it's due.

2. *Having difficulty concentrating*: Being unable to concentrate can result from any of a number of factors, many of which are environmental. Noise, people, a room that's too hot or too cold, and commotion are common causes. Try to find a

location that is free from these distractors or find a way to reduce or eliminate as many of them as possible.

3. *Getting and staying motivated*: When reading, you need to understand why you're reading. Determine if you are skimming, scanning, or reading critically. For example, if you're skimming, don't worry about reading critically. Too, break your reading into manageable parcels. Don't try to read an entire book or twenty articles overnight and expect you'll comprehend and remember everything the next day.

4. *Understanding information that is too difficult*: Find source material you can read and comprehend. This can be particularly important for **research articles** that include lots of statistical information and interpretations. If you're not understanding what you read, try rereading it. If you're still having difficulty, focus on the parts you do understand or find a similar work that's more in line with your ability to comprehend.

5. *Having a limited vocabulary*: Often reading problems stem from having a limited vocabulary, which can make it difficult to understand what you are reading. Developing a strong, robust vocabulary takes time and patience. Writing down new words (and their definitions) that you hear or read each day will help. For jargon and technical terms associated with your topic or subject, keeping a working glossary of unfamiliar terms is also a good idea.

Evaluating the Level of Article Content

One of the primary considerations when selecting articles is the level of content. You want articles that you can understand but that treat the topic in a scholarly, professional way. Magazine articles often provide easy-to-understand content but lack the academic, scholarly emphasis needed for good research. For this reason, most professors will not allow you to use them as part of your research. You can review the information presented in chapters 4 and 7 to help you tell the difference.

Magazine Articles

Because their primary focus is on content that will sell, magazine articles are typically fun, light, leisurely sorts of pieces. The topics and their treatment are generally not scholarly in nature. At best, the articles you read are likely to provide an overview of a given topic but will not provide you with the detailed, accurate information you need as a researcher. In addition, most magazine articles are written by staff writers, who may not know much about the topic. This sometimes translates into misleading or even incorrect information.

Scholarly or Academic Articles

By contrast, scholarly or academic articles are written by professionals who generally have significant knowledge of or working experience with the topic—or both. The goal of these articles isn't to sell the journal but, rather, to provide current, accurate information of interest to professionals and scholars. Many times these articles are based on the original research presented in research articles. Because of the rigorous way these types of articles are researched and produced, they are much preferred over magazine articles dealing with the same topic.

Research Articles

A research article is a scholarly article that essentially reports the results of original, primary research and typically appears in peer-reviewed or refereed periodicals. For this reason, research articles are considered the pinnacle of information sources. Unfortunately, many students struggle with reading research-based articles. Although research articles contain excellent information, many are commonly written at a level or in a way that only people associated with the discipline or topic will understand. Particularly if you have no familiarity with the topic, the vocabulary and concepts alone can be challenging for beginning researchers, not to mention the difficulty of understanding the conclusions drawn by the researcher.

Despite these challenges, you shouldn't arbitrarily dismiss research articles. They contain a wealth of information and can be helpful in directing you to other sources. Moreover, they are almost always written in the same format. Although the format of research articles won't help you to understand the content, it does make them easier to navigate. For example, nonresearch articles, such as literary criticisms, essays, and movie reviews, are generally written in a straight, narrative format set by the author. Research articles, on the other hand, follow a specific pattern, incorporating five standard elements. The sequencing of these elements mirrors the research process. Understanding what these elements are can help you to navigate through research articles more effectively and efficiently. (*Note*: Chapters in scholarly books are also often structured in a similar manner.)

1. *Introduction*: Summarizes the problem researched, its significance, and the nature of the study
2. *Literature review*: Provides a framework for understanding the problem and the theoretical rationale behind conducting the study; sources cited are typically listed at the end in some sort of references page
3. *Methodology*: Describes how the data were collected, including things like the population studied and the data collection instrument used
4. *Results/findings*: Presents a summary of the data collected, typically in the form of charts and tables with accompanying narrative
5. *Discussion/conclusion*: Includes such information as the interpretation of the data, recommendations for further study, and limitations of the study

Other elements you may find in research articles are an abstract or summary, information about the author, and a list of references. The latter can be particularly helpful in directing you to other possible sources of information.

 TIPS

- If you're having difficulty reading or understanding an article, it's probably not a good source for you to use in your research.
- Read the abstract of the article. If you can't understand the summary, you're unlikely to understand the full article.
- Even if you don't read the article itself, examine the article's list of references for possible sources of additional information.

- Read the discussion or conclusion to see what the research revealed. Then, read the rest of the article for more detail or context as needed.
- Research articles often contain charts, graphs, and other visual representations of the data. These will need to be cited if you plan to use them in your final paper.

Evaluating What You Read

As has been noted, just because your search generates results doesn't mean the results will all be useful to you. But, how do you decide which sources are useful and which are not? How will you know which article to use if one says one thing and another seems to say the exact opposite? How can you be sure the information you read is accurate? To answer these and similar questions, you need to have a working knowledge of readability, relevancy, and accuracy.

Readability

As the name implies, **readability** refers to how easy the source is to read. A book may be several hundred pages long. An article may use jargon or other terms you don't understand. This isn't meant to suggest that you should focus on picture books and magazines geared to children. It does, however, mean that you need to find and use sources written at a level and in a way that you can understand.

✔ TIPS

- Using concepts you don't understand won't improve your paper. In fact, most professors will easily pick up on words you don't understand or use properly.
- Quote concepts and terms with which you're unfamiliar.
- As noted earlier, read the abstract. If you can understand the summary, you'll probably be able to understand the article.
- More pages doesn't always equate with better content. Sometimes the shortest articles or books provide the best information.

Relevancy

Relevancy refers to how closely a piece of information aligns with your information needs. Reviewing your topic, purpose statement, and assignment requirements will help you determine the relevance of your sources.

Topic

It goes without saying that your research should produce source material that is in alignment with your topic. However, this doesn't mean that the content of a particular source has to be a direct match to your topic. In fact, related information is often as important as information that's a perfect fit. For example, say your topic deals with means of combating counterfeiting. As part of your research, you find an article about anticounterfeiting activities in Norway. Presumably some of the ways Norwegians combat counterfeiting would be applicable in the United States. You might also find that Norwegians are doing something unique that might (or might not) work here. As a result, even though your focus is on the United States, you might be able to use the article to draw parallels between our country's efforts and those of Norway or even Europe. These sorts of parallels often provide greater context for your topic, thereby giving your arguments much broader scope and emphasis.

Purpose Statement

You also need to look at every source in the context of your purpose statement and research questions. As with your topic, not every source will be in perfect alignment. Still, it's important that every source somehow revolve around, reflect upon, or otherwise contribute to furthering your overall reason or reasons for conducting research in the first place.

Assignment Requirements

Reviewing your assignment is a critical element of determining relevance. Many beginning researchers mistakenly consider only a source's content when determining relevance. However, though certainly important, this approach is far too simplistic. You need to make sure that the source you're considering meets assignment criteria as well. For example, your instructor may require you to use articles from only scholarly or peer-reviewed sources. You might have a whole list of sources that are perfectly aligned with your topic, but if those sources are magazines or websites, you will need to remove them from your list because they don't meet the assignment requirement for scholarly resources.

In reviewing your assignment, be sure your sources—individually and collectively—enable you to meet your assignment's requirements. The following are some of the more common assignment requirements:

Minimum and maximum number of sources: Although some instructors specify a maximum number of sources, it is more common for them to indicate a minimum number of sources you must use.

Level: Some instructors may allow you to use information from sources such as magazines, newspapers, and websites. This is often true in basic, introductory classes. But, as you begin to take upper-level courses, especially in your major, it is increasingly likely that you will be expected to use information from scholarly, peer-reviewed publications.

Date: Often because of a desire to have only the most current information available, your instructor may require you to use sources published within a given range of years. This is especially true of disciplines for which information changes regularly and frequently, such as health care (e.g., nursing) and computer science.

Specificity: There may be a specific source (e.g., textbook) or type of source (e.g., interview) your instructor expects you to use. There might also be a requirement for you to incorporate information from a certain perspective such as gender or culture, a geographic region such as North America, or similar contextual criteria.

Format: Not all information is textual. Increasingly, students are encouraged or even required to incorporate images, charts, and similar nontextual information into their term papers.

Accuracy

Accuracy refers to the degree to which information is true. However, because you're not an expert in the topic, it is sometimes difficult to distinguish between good information and information that is misleading or even incorrect. Even experts in the field sometimes have difficulty making this determination. Doing so is not impossible. It just takes time, patience, and effort. Comparing sources and examining an author's credentials are good starting points for determining the accuracy of the information you've discovered

Compare Sources

The more you read, the more you will begin to see patterns in the information. You will start to see the same thoughts, names, and ideas appearing in multiple sources. These parallels are generally a good thing in that they suggest agreement among those in the know, which, in turn, suggests you're on the right track. However, as noted earlier, just because two sources disagree or seem to contradict one another doesn't mean the information is inaccurate. It may simply be a matter of one author taking a different perspective on the topic than another. Regardless, you need to compare sources along a number of dimensions to determine accuracy. Some of these elements are summarized here.

> *Bias*: Just because a source is clearly biased doesn't necessarily mean the information it contains is incorrect. You just need to determine which is fact and which is a matter of perspective. As a rule, biased sources provide a misleading view of a subject and prevent you from seeing alternative perspectives and possible research pathways to explore. For those reasons alone, you should generally strive to locate sources that provide a balanced approach to your topic.

> *Date*: Some topics are affected more by date of publication than others. For example, because of new discoveries and developments, computer science changes continuously, whereas philosophy is relatively stable. Still, sources shouldn't be removed from your list just because they're old. Old sources are good for providing context and for showing the evolution of an idea.

Audience: Information geared toward college students or professionals is generally preferred to lower-level sources. Although it may provide good information, an article written for an elementary school child probably isn't appropriate for a college-level term paper. Age, gender, educational level, socioeconomic status, and ethnicity are among the many elements helping to determine the audience.

References: Because they place their claims into context, sources containing a list of references or a bibliography are generally stronger than those that do not. Such lists also provide additional sources that you might use as part of your paper.

Examine the Author's Credentials

Looking at the author's credentials can help you determine whether she is qualified to write on the topic. An article about dinosaurs written by a paleontologist, for example, is likely to be more credible and contain more detailed, accurate information than an article written by a ten-year-old boy. This is not to say the boy's article can't or doesn't contain good information. However, it is far more likely that the information written by someone who works in the profession will be more current, accurate, and insightful.

Unfortunately, determining whether someone is an authority on the topic or merely a person with an interest in it isn't always easy. Scholarly, professional publications will often (but not always) provide information about the author's education, professional experience, and previous research and publications on the topic. On the other hand, magazines, newspapers, and other nonacademic types of publications often provide little or no information about the author. In fact, many such articles don't have identifiable authors because they were written by staff members employed by the publication.

✓ TIPS

- When you find a useful information source, do an author search on the authors listed to determine if they have published additional books or articles. The more an individual has published on a subject—particularly in academic journals and books—the more likely it is that the information is dependable.

- When accuracy cannot be determined or is questionable, you should use the source sparingly if at all.
- Just because an author's name isn't provided doesn't mean the article is any less accurate than any other article.

Reliability versus Validity

Although you may not be using research articles often, when you do, it will help you to be aware of two specific concepts related to accuracy: *reliability* and *validity*. Understanding these concepts will help you to better evaluate the value of the research.

Reliability refers to the degree to which a test consistently measures whatever is being measured. For example, let's say researcher 1 performs an experiment and researcher 2 performs exactly the same experiment. The data produced will be considered reliable to the degree that they are the same each time the experiment is performed. Reliability is always expressed as a coefficient ranging from 0 (no reliability) to 1 (perfect reliability). This number often appears in the abstract or results section of research articles. It is also likely to be found in a table or chart along with other relevant statistical data. (*Note*: A reliability coefficient can be calculated from only measurable, quantifiable data. It does not apply to nonquantitative types of research, such as literary criticism or historical research.)

The following are some factors that contribute to producing unreliable data:

- Questions that are ambiguous or unclear
- Procedures of test administration that vary or are not standardized
- Study participants who are fatigued or nervous
- Study participants who misinterpret questions or guess

In a research article, **validity** essentially refers to the accuracy of the results. It is the extent to which the data deal with or reflect the topic being studied. It does not refer to the instruments used to collect the data but, rather, to the interpretations of the scores obtained from the instruments.

Validity is best thought of in terms of degree. As with reliability, validity is associated with only measurable, quantifiable research.

Poor validity can result from any of a number of factors, including the following:

- Data collection instrument doesn't measure what it's supposed to measure
- Incorrect analysis of data or data patterns
- Unclear directions or confusing administration of data collection tool
- Poorly designed questions or measures of variables
- Inconsistent or subjective scoring methods

☑ TIPS

- Data can be reliable without being valid.
- Data cannot be both valid and unreliable.
- Reliability is necessary but not sufficient for validity.
- A valid test is always reliable, but a reliable test is not necessarily valid.

Understanding Disagreement among Sources

As you read, it is rare that all sources will be in 100 percent agreement. You might read something that seems to disagree with or even contradict something you've already read. Disagreement among or between sources isn't uncommon, nor does it mean one source is right and one is wrong. Each needs to be understood for what it is. Especially for argumentative papers, finding contradictory sources is actually helpful in that it presents you with an opposing viewpoint you need to address. Regardless, rather than arbitrarily casting aside such sources, you need to determine why there's a discrepancy. At that point, you can decide whether to incorporate those sources into your paper and, if so, in what ways. The following are some ways to understand disagreement:

1. *Context*: Recognize that all information exists in context. Culture, gender, ethnicity, age, geography, and other factors can impact how a topic is researched as well as how authors write about it. When you read something that disagrees with something else, check the text for contextual factors that might have influenced how the information is being presented or discussed.

2. *Dated information*: Sometimes information is not wrong; it is simply dated. The information may have been correct at the time it was published only to subsequently become wrong in light of new, more recent discoveries. If your topic is time-sensitive, you will have to decide whether using a book from 1985 is better than using no book at all. Conversely, if historical context is important or if you are doing a term paper examining the historical development of a topic or idea, a book from 1985 might be ideal in that it provides information produced during the time you're researching.

3. *Different definitions*: How key terms are defined by the author can also result in disagreement. For example, one author might define *student success* as getting an A while another might define it simply as not failing. Both are right, or, perhaps more accurately, neither is incorrect. They've simply defined *success* differently, and, therefore, how they write about success will differ accordingly. On a related note, sometimes definitions are simply weak or even unacceptable. In these instances, it is hard to make good quality comparisons between sources. They may not be in disagreement as much as they are simply talking about two different topics or ideas altogether.

4. *Different interpretations*: This is essentially the classic question of whether the cup is half empty or half full. Sometimes there is an honest difference that results from the interpretation of the data. However, many times authors simply vary in their interpretations. One author might say 51 percent agree with his standpoint while another might say that 49 percent disagree with hers. Both are saying the same thing, but how the information is presented reflects the author's interpretation.

5. *The presence of bias*: Bias is essentially a lack of balance. Purposely or otherwise, the information is skewed in one direction more than others. Most associate bias with authors who inject their personal values and beliefs into the information being presented. For example, a Democrat is likely to have a different perspective on the presidential campaign than a Republican. However, bias also results when an author fails to include significant facts or key arguments. Whatever the reason for the bias, knowing its source and its direction helps to put information into its proper context.

Recognizing Errors in Reasoning

Although editors make every effort to eliminate wrong or inaccurate information, sometimes incorrect or misleading information is published. And though it is important to read critically, it is even more important to resist the temptation to criticize unfairly. As you read, you need to be able to judge the various claims an author makes to determine whether those claims are accurate. This includes analyzing the claims made by the author as well as the logic and structure of his statements and arguments to see if they make sense.

Watch for errors in reasoning, or fallacies. A **fallacy** is a statement or argument based on a false assumption or incorrect reasoning that avoids, confuses, or oversimplifies a point. Researchers often commit fallacies in their writing. Recognizing them as you read can help you to gauge the relative accuracy of the claims being made. Conversely, as you write your paper, you should strive to avoid using such errors to make or support your points. Your paper will be much stronger if you do. The following are some common fallacies:

- *Red herring/changing the subject*: Introduces or uses irrelevant or distracting points

    Example: Why worry about drunk drivers when the federal government is funding abortions?

- *Name-calling/ad hominem/personal attack*: Tries to focus on and discredit, or generate mistrust of, the person or group (rather than the issue)

    Example: We shouldn't listen to those who want to ban the Lord's Prayer before a sporting event because they're all atheists.

- *Straw man*: Oversimplifies or distorts other people's arguments or attributes views to them they don't hold while ignoring valid arguments

    Example: People who think marijuana should be legalized have no respect for the law.

- *Post hoc fallacy/false cause*: Contends that because something happened first, it must have caused something else

    Example: Teen pregnancy has increased since sex education was introduced in school.

- *Appeal to popularity/bandwagon appeal*: Suggests if a large enough number believe in something, it must be true or valid

    Example: Is abortion wrong? One hundred million Christians can't be wrong!

- *Appeal to ignorance*: Maintains that being unable to prove something wrong implies that it is right (based on the notion of an opponent's being unable to *dis*prove a conclusion)

    Example: Bigfoot exists because no one has been able to prove otherwise.

- *Slippery slope argument*: States that one thing inevitably leads to other, more serious things (e.g., marijuana leads to harder drugs)

    Example: If the government funds abortion, next it will support assisted suicide and then murder!

- *Hasty generalization*: Uses a small, limited sample to generate a conclusion about a large, general population

Example: The first six individuals voted for a Republican. Therefore, it's likely a Republican will be elected.

- *Appeal to authority/testimonial*: Uses a famous or respected individual's association as an endorsement of the quality of the product or idea

    Example: This diet must work because it's endorsed by "famous actress," and she's thin.

Evaluating Websites

When evaluating websites, you should consider all the preceding fallacies. However, some additional elements you need to consider when deciding whether to use a website are outlined in the following sections.

Accessibility

As design technology advances, many page features may not appear or function properly on different browsers or on older versions of the same browser. Some may also require the installation of software updates or additional software for full functionality. This does not mean the information on such sites is any less useful than that on others; sometimes the reverse may be true. However, because of the extra time and effort needed to get to the information, you may wish to reduce or eliminate such sites from your research in favor of sites that are more consistently accessible or that have greater accessibility.

Authentication

Authentication is an accessibility issue unto itself in that some sites protect their content by blocking unauthorized users. Online versions of professional journals, for example, often require membership or a fee-based account in order to access journal content. Many libraries, though, provide free access to content from these sites. If you do decide to pay or to create an account for yourself, read through the agreement. On the plus side, you may be able to join the sponsoring organization and gain access to the journal (and other amenities) for the same price as subscribing to the journal itself. On the downside, you may become liable for costs such as additional fees and automatic renewals.

Links to Other Sites

It is natural to assume that the more sites which are linked, the more useful a site becomes. However, this isn't necessarily true. When links are provided, check whether they're relevant, current, and functional. At the very least, they should reflect the content of the page and not link to sites or services that have nothing to do with the topic. Conversely, sites that do not link to other sites or that link to only other pages or sites maintained by the site's author should be used with caution as the information they contain will often be highly subjective or biased.

Organization

Is the page organized well? For example, are there buttons taking you to the top of the page or elsewhere within the page? Are navigation bars or tools available? An author who has taken the time to incorporate these features is generally more concerned about researchers getting to the information than is someone who hasn't.

Publisher/Host

Try to determine who hosts the site or page you're reading. As noted earlier, just because the information comes from a .edu or .gov site doesn't make it any more legitimate than information from a .com site. Determining who is responsible for monitoring content and verifying whether the site is fully sanctioned by the hosting institution are key to revealing a site's focus and possible bias.

Readability

Pages with excessive graphics, frames, and other distractions often make it difficult to find what you're looking for. Pages with features such as a coordinated color scheme and standard fonts will generally be easier to read than pages that appear thrown together.

UNDERSTANDING URLS

A discussion about evaluating the relevancy and accuracy of websites would not be complete without talking about how websites are arranged and how this can lead to confusion and otherwise compromise the search for good information.

As you are probably aware, every site on the Web has a unique address or Uniform Resource Locator (URL) consisting of a series of numbers. However, that series of numbers is meaningless to the average user. So, to make things easier, all web addresses also have a converted text address. The following two addresses provide a good example. Even though the second is more familiar, both URLs will take you to the same Environmental Protection Agency website.

http://134.67.21.34
http://epa.gov

A website's domain defines the type of control or authority of the website and is used to assign addresses. Typically, a site's domain is the last segment or suffix of the address. Standard domains are represented by a three-letter combination. Some URLs might also be represented by a two-letter country code (e.g., au = Australia, ca = Canada). The following are examples of some standard domains:

.com .... commercial

.edu .... education

.net .... network

.gov .... U.S. government

.org .... organization

.mil .... U.S. military

.ca .... Canada

.info .... information

.eu .... European Union

Continued on next page

Continued from previous page

When deciding to use websites as part of their research, many students mistakenly believe that information found on certain domains is better or less biased than information found on other domains. That is, when forced to choose, most people would typically select information from a .edu (education) site before that found on a .com (commercial) site. The idea is that an educational facility's site is more likely to contain balanced and accurate information than is a site geared toward sales.

However, this distinction is not necessarily helpful. First, you cannot assume that information from one domain is inherently any better than that found on any other. Second, the domain essentially reflects where the information is stored; it says little, if anything, about the origin of such information. A student could essentially be running her own website using the campus's .edu domain. This doesn't mean her site is educational or that the university sanctions the student's site. It merely means the site is stored or hosted on a computer at the university.

Instead of examining a site's URL, try to determine the site's sponsor or author and use that information to evaluate the site. That approach will provide you with far greater insight into the context and origins of the page than will knowing the computer on which it is stored.

Stability of Information

Sites that don't incorporate a "last updated" notification should be used with caution. Knowing when a page was last updated places its content in context. It also demonstrates how much attention the publisher is giving to the site. That said, frequent updating isn't necessarily good. It may demonstrate a lack of knowledge on a topic in that the publisher may simply be correcting mistakes and not adding new content.

Style and Tone

Misspelled words, errors in grammar and punctuation, and the tone or wording of a site can detract from readability and reliability. If the author of a page or site doesn't take the time to correct these simple errors, ensuring the accuracy of content likely isn't taking place either.

? REFLECTIONS

- Go to the website for People for the Ethical Treatment of Animals (PETA.org). Then, open another window and access the National Milk Producers Federation (NMPF.org). Both are .org sites, designating them as being sponsored by a nonprofit organization. What are some of the differences you can find—stated or implied—between each group's perspectives on milk, dairy cows, and the dairy industry?

- Use a search tool and conduct a search on a topic of interest. From the list of results, rank three articles in terms of their relevancy.

- Describe a scenario in which either readability, relevancy, or accuracy would be more important to you than the other two concepts. How? Why? What would cause this to change?

- Examine two sources on the same topic. Which one (if either) do you think is more accurate? In what ways? If there is no discernible difference, how are they alike?

- Using the considerations for evaluating websites listed earlier in this chapter, locate two websites on the same topic. Rate them using 2 = high, 1 = low, and 0 = none or does not apply. Which site is best?

CHAPTER 11

Conducting Ethically and
Legally Responsible Research

W hen writing your term paper, you will rely heavily on the books, articles, websites, and other sources of information generated by others. That's perfectly acceptable and an expected part of the research process. However, you can't simply include the thoughts and ideas of others without giving them credit. You also cannot submit their ideas as your own. Doing either is a form of theft and has serious academic and legal consequences. To avoid those, it is essential that you maintain a complete and accurate record of each source of information that you use. Through a variety of techniques, you can then incorporate these details into your paper to help ensure you've used the information from a given source in an appropriate manner—both ethically and legally.

Some Basic Concepts

To better understand the ethical and legal issues surrounding the use of information, you need to understand three interrelated concepts. They all revolve around the basic notion of someone creating something and maintaining legal rights to it. As a researcher, you must recognize these rights and acknowledge the originator when you write your term paper.

Intellectual Property

As the term suggests, **intellectual property** (IP) essentially refers to property created through the use of the mind (i.e., intellect). Authors, musicians, artists, and inventors are some of the primary producers of IP. The concept encompasses a wide variety of original creations, including manuscripts, artwork, inventions, performances, and designs.

Citation

A citation is a trail leading readers back to the original source of information and gives credit to the author or authors. What's included in a citation—what is cited—and how vary depending on the discipline. Author, page number, date of publication, and title are examples of the types of information contained in a typical citation. Citations appear in your narrative and refer to a list of sources located at the end.

Plagiarism

When you commit **plagiarism**, you've essentially stolen the intellectual property of another. This happens when you fail to properly cite the work of others or submit the work of someone else as your own. To avoid plagiarism, you need to do your own work and properly acknowledge any information you use that's not your own.

Why Cite?

Many beginning researchers question the need to cite sources or don't understand why it's important. Admittedly, doing so can be a tedious, time-consuming task. There are all sorts of guidelines and rules you need to follow, and as a result, many students fail to provide complete citations or accurate citations. However, at the most basic level, citations serve as signposts, directing readers to sources of information. As a simple example, say you read an article and a particular passage mentions the work of Smith. Because Smith's work seems to be in perfect alignment with your topic, answering key questions and filling in gaps in understanding, you're eager to acquire the complete source to read more.

Now, imagine your frustration at not being able to do so. Lacking a citation, you don't even know if the item is a book, an article, or something else, and you have no way of tracking it down. You also don't know whether the information was produced last month or last century. You may not even know Smith's first name to try to isolate his (or her) research from that of all the other Smiths out there.

In addition to leading readers to sources of information, citing sources is important for other reasons, including the following:

Developing professional credibility: If others cite your work, you will receive greater recognition for the work you've done and the contribution you've made to the discipline.

Establishing responsibility for information: Without a citation, it is assumed that any information you've produced is yours and that it is accurate. In turn, this makes you culpable for consequences—positive or negative—that result from your work. A positive scenario is outlined in the preceding point. However, in cases where you have supplied false or misleading information, you might be held legally liable for the consequences.

Determining validity of information: Without a citation, you can't check the original source of the information to determine if it's true or current or if it even exists in the first place.

Avoiding plagiarism: You need to properly cite sources to distinguish between your work and that of others in order to avoid committing plagiarism.

What to Cite?

How do you know when to cite something and when *not* to cite something? What *not* to cite is a little easier to define. Among other things, you don't need to cite (a) easily observable information (e.g., grass is green), (b) commonly known facts (e.g., the Declaration of Independence was signed in 1776), or (c) common sayings that have no clear owner (e.g., "Tomorrow starts today").

What to cite, though, is more problematic. The simple answer is that you should cite anything that's not your own thought or idea—anything you didn't know before reading the material. Even so, that's not always an easy distinction to make. For example, what is common knowledge to you may not be to someone else. In the end, if you're in doubt, cite it!

Incorporating Text

Summarizing, paraphrasing, and **quoting** are three techniques you can use to properly incorporate source material into your paper without committing plagiarism. Each has advantages and disadvantages. Figure 11.1 provides an explanation of each technique along with guidelines for using each and common errors to avoid. You need to decide which technique is best for the information you wish to use and how you wish to present it. A good paper usually presents information using all three techniques.

FIGURE 11.1

Three Techniques for Incorporating Information

Incorporate Information by ...	In Order to ...	Guidelines	Common Errors
Summarizing *Rewriting and condensing original source material to present main ideas in a narrower, more focused way*	Focus by eliminating extra information Simplify or condense source Make a minor point when you write	Provide a citation Change the order in which ideas appear Quote exact wordings Write entirely in your own words Use wording and sentence structure different from original Do not include interpretation or analysis	Not summarizing fairly Presenting minor points as major points and vice versa Not using your own words and sentence structure Not adding your own ideas or interpretations

Continued on next page

Continued from previous page

Incorporate Information by ...	In Order to ...	Guidelines	Common Errors
Paraphrasing *Using roughly the same amount of words as the original to restate information without quoting it*	Arrange, simplify, or clarify material Normalize your writing so that all of your writing is the same Provide more detail than a summary	Provide a citation Write using mostly your own words Use wording and sentence structure different from original Put quotation marks around words or phrases you do use from the original Do not include interpretation or analysis	Changing only a few words Keeping the same sentence structure and order of presentation Adding ideas, analysis, interpretation, or explanation Adding an assessment Misrepresenting what was actually said
Quoting *Using the exact wording and formatting of the original*	Include another's words that are stronger or better than yours Provide evidence of support of your views Provide historical flavor or context Provide a specific example Express technical language or terms To distance yourself from the quote Present material for analysis To comment on the quoted material	Provide a citation Surround quoted material with quotation marks ("quote"). Duplicate the *exact* wording, including punctuation and formatting Use an ellipsis (...) to designate omitted words Avoid perception of padding by using long quotes	Not including your ideas Heavily quoting one source more than others Using excessively long quotes Quoting a source quoted by someone else Not providing a context for the quote Changing the meaning or intent of the original by omitting words

Examples

The following paragraph will be used to provide examples of each technique:

The amount and variety of information have grown exponentially in recent years. Because of this, many people experience *information overload*. The term was coined in 1970 and essentially refers to one's being overcome by too much information. There are a number of things people can do to overcome or at least diminish information overload in their lives. Focusing on gaining information we need to know versus information that's nice to know and focusing on quality over quantity are good starting points. Single-tasking—keeping your mind focused on one issue at a time—is another. One way to gain this focus is by spending parts of each day disconnected from interruptions (e.g., switching off e-mail, phones, social media).

Quote: The author observes that "the amount and variety of information have grown exponentially in recent years."

Summary: The amount and variety of information cause many individuals to experience "information overload." The author presents some basic strategies that can be used to help overcome the latter.

Paraphrase: There are many ways to help address the "information overload" some people experience in today's information-rich world. Focusing on the quality of information (versus the quantity) is one method. In addition, although there is a lot of information we might find interesting, focusing on that which is most needed is critical. Concentrating on one thing at a time and reducing time spent on distractions such as e-mail and social media can also be helpful in this regard.

Paraphrasing versus Summarizing

Most students generally understand how to quote material. When they try to summarize or paraphrase material, however, difficulties typically start to arise. For example, many students mistakenly believe that simply changing words or the order of words is paraphrasing. They might substitute "cops" for "police" and "jail" for "prison." Having done so, they believe they have paraphrased the information and no longer need to quote it. Unfortunately, merely changing words or the order in which they appear is not sufficient. It is not paraphrasing. It is plagiarism. Figure 11.2 characterizes some of the key similarities and differences between summarized and paraphrased material.

FIGURE 11.2

Similarities and Differences between Summaries and Paraphrases

Summaries	Paraphrases
• Report your understanding to reader • Can be any length • Select and condense main ideas and concepts • May arrange points in any order • Explain, sometimes interpret • Should be accurate and complete	• Report your understanding to reader • Tend to be rather short • Record each point • Present points in original order • Include no interpretation • Should be complete and make sense on their own without misleading or misrepresenting

☑ TIPS

- Read the passage several times, jotting down the main ideas. Then outline the passage and rearrange the outline.
- Write the paraphrase without looking at the original. Then compare it to the original to be sure you've maintained meaning.
- Your paraphrase should sound like you, using your vocabulary and writing style, enabling a reader to recognize the work as your own (i.e., not the work of someone else).
- Quote exact words or phrases you did not change but intend to use.

Elements of a Citation

Two different elements are required for a complete citation. The first—an **in-text citation**—alerts the reader to material you've acquired from another source. The second—a list of sources—provides full attribution information for all the sources cited in your narrative.

In-Text Citations

When you quote individuals or use information generated by others, you need to give them credit. Appropriate citation information (e.g., author's name, year of publication) is typically provided within the text of the document. However, it is important to note that exactly what information is required and how it is presented vary depending on the citation style being used.

List of Sources

The second element of a citation is a list of referenced sources at the end of your paper. That is, the last part of your paper will be a bibliography or list of all the sources you've cited in your paper.

Citation Style

If a citation is a reference to another's work that you've used, the *citation style* is the approved, standardized way cited information is to be formatted and incorporated into your paper. The elements of a citation are fairly common regardless of the style. However, because each discipline emphasizes different information in a citation, how citation information appears will vary depending on the style used. Four of the more common styles you're likely to encounter and their associated disciplines are summarized in the following list:

APA (American Psychological Association): Psychology, education, and the other social sciences

Chicago: History as well as nonscholarly books, journals, and newspapers

MLA (Modern Language Association of America): Literature, the arts, and the humanities

Turabian: A composite style (derived from Chicago) for use with every discipline

Citation Style Guide

A *style guide* is the written document or book that details a citation style's formatting expectations and rules. Most libraries and writing centers have copies of style manuals for you to use to generate your citations. Your instructor may or may not require you to use a specific citation style. When given the choice, you should use the one most closely associated with your major program of study.

Unfortunately, as there are dozens of styles, it is far beyond the scope of this book to give an example of every possible citation style and format. It is equally impossible to show examples for every type of citation (e.g., book, article by two authors, government document). You should always refer to the appropriate style guide to determine how to construct a proper citation. The following sections, though, provide a visual representation of some of the similarities and differences between the APA and MLA styles. Both styles cite Claude Badley's book *Lion Around*, published by Big Cat Press in 2012.

APA

Introduce the source in your paper in one of the following ways:

Badley (2012) observes . . .

or

It has been stated (Badley, 2012) that . . .

Use the following format for your Reference List:

Badley, C. (2012). *Lion around.* Omaha, NE: Big Cat Press.

MLA

Introduce the source in your paper in one of the following ways:

Badley (25) recounts . . .

or

It has been stated (Badley 25) that . . .

Use the following style for your Works Cited section:

> Badley, Claude. *Lion Around.* Omaha, NE: Big Cat Press, 2012.
> Print.

Notes

Some citation styles use notes to provide more detail on the content without drawing attention away from the primary text. Such notes appear either as **footnotes** (at the bottom of the page) or as **endnotes** (at the end of a chapter, section, or entire work). In the body of your paper, use the following style to indicate additional explanation or comment:

> Badley notes the need for caution.[1]

In this case, the superscript 1 refers to either footnote 1 or endnote 1. Footnotes are formatted at the bottom of the page on which the reference occurs (see example below), and endnotes appear in a Notes section at the end of your paper. Most styles that use such notation encourage the use of endnotes rather than footnotes so as not to overly distract the reader. In either case, the note might appear like this:

---

1. Badley suffered major scrapes and contusions on his last photography expedition, nearly losing his camera (and his leg!) to a female lion.

Bibliography

Sometimes referred to as a *bibliography* or *works cited* or *reference list* page, the last section of your paper will be a list of the sources you used to construct your paper. The important point is that it's not a list of all the sources you've consulted. It's a listing of those you've actually used. That is, if you cite a work in your paper, it should be included in your list of references. This is true regardless of how much content you incorporated or the length of the original source material. As part of your paper or as a separate assignment, some instructors may ask you to annotate your list. This involves writing a brief summary of the source and your personal insights and thoughts on such. Similarly, some instructors may ask you to provide a ranked list along with justification for how or why each source was useful to you.

- Remove the hyperlink functionality from copied and pasted hyperlinks to ensure they appear and print out like the other sources in your list.
- Because no citation software is 100 percent accurate, you are responsible for the content of your bibliography and how it appears.

Plagiarism
· · · · · · · · · ·

As noted earlier, plagiarism is essentially the improper use of another's ideas or work. How instructors and institutions deal with plagiarism varies. In part, it depends on which type of plagiarism was committed, how much, how often, and the severity of such. Still, it is important to note that any plagiarism of any kind is a serious offense and is not treated lightly. Plagiarism can be characterized in three different ways.

Intentional plagiarism: The deliberate stealing of another's ideas or representing such as your own.

Unintentional plagiarism: Results from factors such as a lack of knowledge of proper source use, a misunderstanding of the rules of citation, or careless note taking.

Self-recycling: Using the same paper or project for multiple purposes. For example, you have two term papers due in the same semester. To save time and effort, you write one paper and submit it in both classes.

Reasons to Avoid Plagiarism

Because so much information is available so readily, many students don't consider plagiarism to be a form of cheating or stealing. They see nothing wrong about copying and pasting text into a paper and not providing a citation for such.

Academic Consequences

Each instructor and institution has different guidelines for dealing with those who are found guilty of plagiarism. Plagiarism typically results in suspension from the class, automatic failure, or even dismissal from the institution, among other penalties. Such an outcome obviously impacts your academic career but will also likely have ramifications for financial aid, career plans, athletic eligibility, and more, to say nothing of the embarrassment you will cause yourself, your family, and your friends.

Cheating Yourself

The ability to process information is critical for living in the information age. By plagiarizing, you may not develop the skills needed to succeed in graduate school or your chosen profession. If you're found guilty of plagiarism, it is unlikely that you'll be admitted to graduate school or another form of post-baccalaureate education.

Easily Detected

Be aware that just as plagiarism is easy to commit, it's also easy to detect. When a student's writing style suddenly changes in the middle of a page, that's a pretty obvious and clear sign that work has been copied from someone else. Too, various plagiarism-detection software packages and services have simplified the process of finding plagiarized passages.

Diminishes the Value of Your Degree

When you receive a grade, it implies that you've done the work. If you don't do the work, you'll never know what you're capable of achieving or, in turn, whether your degree is worth the paper it's printed on.

Reduces Your Credibility

Plagiarism is like crying wolf. Once you've committed plagiarism, your instructors are likely to scrutinize your work more heavily in the future or simply be reluctant to accept work from you as your own.

Impacts the Grading Curve

Plagiarized work can skew the grading curve. It's simply in your best interest if all students do their own work to avoid inflated grades.

Term Paper Mills

Online **term paper mills** (also called simply *paper mills*) are a relatively recent phenomenon. These are websites that sell term papers, admission application essays, and more. Most promise such services as "custom-written papers on any subject by any deadline for any level of student." Some even go so far as to promise the grade you'll receive. Many times the documents have already been prepared, and you're simply purchasing someone else's work. Other times you can have a paper written for you. Pricing is based on a number of criteria, such as level of writing, expected grade, assignment deadline, and type of writing (e.g., term paper, essay).

UNDER NO CIRCUMSTANCES IS IT APPROPRIATE

TO PURCHASE OR SUBMIT

ONE OF THESE PAPERS AS YOUR OWN!

Why? It's plagiarism, plain and simple. Don't be fooled by sites promising their papers are "plagiarism free." This is a very narrow view of plagiarism and an extremely dubious claim. Even *if* all the paper's sources are properly cited (i.e., plagiarism free), you're still submitting a paper that someone else has written and, therefore, are guilty of committing plagiarism by submitting such as your own.

The following is a direct quote and is typical of paper mills' responses to the question, "Can you assure me that my paper is plagiarism free?"

> We check each order with our advanced anti-plagiarism software to ensure that your paper is 100% original. With our commitment to quality and zero tolerance policy for plagiarism, you can relax knowing we will meet your needs. We will terminate any writer who violates these terms. (Academia Help, www.academiahelp.com/faq.php)

It's important to point out that if "advanced anti-plagiarism software" is available to this company, it's also available to your instructors. Even without software, plagiarism is often easy to detect. With software? Even more so.

? REFLECTIONS

- What is the citation style associated with your topic? With your discipline?

- Determine whether your library has the corresponding style guide(s) for your topic and discipline.

- Examine the way an article by one author is cited using one citation style and compare it to the same citation using a second style. What similarities and differences do you notice?

- Use the following paragraphs to practice quoting, paraphrasing, and summarizing (examples follow the reading).

> *Canis lupus.* Timberwolf. Grey wolf. By whatever name they are called, wolves are arguably one of Mother Nature's most misunderstood and maligned creatures. Children's stories, for example, abound with "evilized" images of snarling, frothing wolves, intent on causing mischief or harm. "The Big, Bad Wolf" of *Three Little Pigs'* fame even threatens to kill and eat the main protagonists of the story!
>
> Whether the cause or the result of children's stories, the negative images most people have of wolves are not restricted to bedtime stories. Unlike "man's best friend"—a direct descendent of wolves—throughout history, wolves have been treated with fear and hostility. As a result, in many places throughout the world, they have been hunted to near extinction. In turn, the absence of this key, natural predator has caused many other animal populations to soar (e.g., deer), sometimes to the point where special hunts are held to cull the number to a manageable level.
>
> As with all myths, there is no doubt some grain of truth to the wolf's reputation. Has livestock been killed by a wolf? Certainly. But, for the most part, these cases are the exceptions, not the rule. Moreover, they are perfectly understandable when seen in context. Basically, because of diminished habitat and the resultant decrease in available sources of food, we shouldn't be surprised to learn of a wolf attacking livestock in order to survive. Unfortunately, it seems

certain that many wolves are killed simply because they are perceived as a potential threat, not for having actually killed any livestock.

Quote (words exactly as they appear in the original):

"The negative images most people have of wolves are not restricted to bedtime stories."

Summary (a sentence or so stating the main idea for each paragraph):

Wolves are misunderstood. Many of the causes for the various misperceptions about wolves likely have some basis in fact but do not provide sufficient evidence for the wolf's negative reputation. When wolves attack livestock, it is often because the wolves lack natural food sources. Conversely, "prey species" populations often rise significantly as wolf populations decline.

Paraphrase (more detail than a summary):

Many people fear wolves or have negative impressions of them. Because of the wolf's "bad" reputation, the species has been hunted extensively. There are many reasons behind the wolf's image problem, including occasional attacks on livestock. However, when you consider habitat destruction and reductions in natural sources of food, these occasional attacks are not surprising. They are a necessity if the wolf is to survive.

CHAPTER 12

Writing Your Paper

. . . .

You have researched, acquired, and evaluated information, and it is now time to put together the actual paper. It is beyond the scope of this book to detail exactly how this is to be accomplished. That is, the point here is not to provide a grammar guide or otherwise instruct you about how to write a research paper. For that, you should refer to an introductory composition text or visit your campus's writing center. Rather, the purpose of this chapter is to make you aware of some of the common challenges at this stage and to provide strategies to assist you with respect to the writing process.

Review Your Assignment
. . . .

As this book began, so it ends. First and foremost, before you begin writing your paper, you need to carefully review your assignment to ensure you're able to meet all the assignment's criteria. Key among the things to look for is whether you have the right number as well as the right kinds of sources. For example, if you were asked to use a minimum of ten sources, you need to be certain you have at least that many. Likewise, if you were not allowed to use websites as sources, you need to be sure you haven't done so. Meeting assignment requirements won't necessarily ensure a better grade, but it will help you to avoid losing points simply because you overlooked or forgot to address a specific requirement.

Manage Writing Anxiety

Many symptoms of writing anxiety can produce stress or otherwise cause students to delay writing. Among other challenges, writing may be difficult, or you may simply not want to write your paper. You may feel self-conscious or worry that you won't be able to express yourself well. You may not know where to begin, or you might have trouble just getting started. These and a host of similar concerns can result in anxiety and discomfort. Unfortunately, there is no cure-all. Moreover, how one person overcomes her writing anxiety may not work for you. However, a few general suggestions apply to everyone who might be experiencing writing anxiety.

- Resign yourself to the fact that you have to write your paper.
- Instead of trying to write your paper in one long, marathon session, break the writing up into smaller, more manageable components.
- Don't worry about producing the perfect paper on your first try. Complete your initial draft and revise it later.
- Stretch, breathe deeply, and try to remain relaxed throughout the process. If you have some sort of ritual or activity that puts you in the right frame of mind (e.g., drinking tea), by all means use it!
- Read aloud what you write, maybe even to a friend or family member. You (and he or she) will often hear things you didn't catch by only silently reading what you've written.

Examine Your Skill Set

Some professors are stricter than others with respect to grammar, writing style, and similar structural concerns. Regardless, if you struggle or are at all uncomfortable with any of the following, you need to be honest with yourself and consider seeking assistance early in the writing process. Otherwise, be sure to budget enough time to not only complete each of the following tasks but also go back and make corrections as needed.

Typing

If you're a slow or inaccurate typist, or both, you might want to consider hiring someone to type your paper for you. On the plus side, you will save yourself considerable time and aggravation. On the negative side, you'll need to have your paper written *exactly* as you want it to be typed. Many typists don't, won't, or even can't proofread. If they do, they typically charge an extra (sometimes costly) fee. Most typists simply agree to type your paper as is, including errors you've made.

Formatting

Most students are proficient with basic word processing. Many, though, lack a working familiarity with some of the upper-level functionality of whatever software they're using. Although there is a slight learning curve, a small, up-front investment of time learning how to use some of these more advanced features, such as page numbering, image formatting, and citation tools, may save you considerable time over the course of typing your paper and help you avoid last-minute stress and problems.

Citing

Do you know which citation style you're to use? If one isn't specified for your assignment, do you know the one used by your discipline? For many students, citing their sources can be a very time-consuming and frustrating process. Some professors are more meticulous than others in terms of how closely they want you to follow the citation style you're using. Others won't care as long as you're consistent. Most fall somewhere in between. Be aware that there are many websites and software packages that claim to generate citation information. Many do a better-than-average job. However, be aware that no citation software or website will be 100 percent accurate all the time. Whether you choose to input citation information yourself or use some sort of automated method for doing so, you are responsible for providing complete and correct citations.

Proofreading

Bad writing doesn't mean that you didn't do the work or that your research efforts were poor. Your instructor understands that you're not a professional writer. However, things like typographical and grammatical errors can significantly detract from the overall impression your paper makes. Simply put, in the age of word processors, with spell checker and grammar checker being standard on most mainstream word-processing software, there's no excuse for incorrect spellings or bad grammar. As with citation software, be aware that no word-processing software will catch every mistake.

✅ TIPS

- Budget additional time for any and all of the preceding skills with which you're not comfortable or not proficient.
- Have someone else with good writing and editing skills (re)read each copy of your paper for errors and clarity.
- Contact your campus's tutoring or writing center for assistance with writing your paper and citing your sources.

Master the Writing Process

The process of writing a research paper is different from that for creative writing. At the very least, when writing creatively, you're telling a story that may or may not be true. Facts follow one after the other in the order in which you want them to be revealed. Admittedly, research writing also tells a story, but it does so by supporting each concept or idea with evidence from other sources. It is a written analysis, combining all your thoughts and information into a single whole. Starting with an overall thesis or premise, the "story" moves forward with each successive piece of evidence being presented in a logical, systematic, and coherent way. Each successive thought builds upon previous ideas and supports the paper's overall thesis or purpose. Each thought also contributes to and provides context for subsequent points and evidence.

✅ TIPS

- *Write!* Don't make excuses. Just start writing. Don't worry about grammar and spelling (too much) at this stage. At least initially, the focus should be on getting your thoughts and ideas down in some kind of logical order. Proofreading will come later.

- Write a little bit each day. Stay focused and write as much as you can for as long as you can. But don't overdo it. Know your limits. By breaking the project into smaller portions, you're likely to struggle less in the long run.

Get Organized

Organizing and writing about all the source material you've collected can be one of the most daunting aspects of the entire research process. It is important not to produce a paper that is nothing more than a series of quotes or copied and pasted text. Rather, your narrative should flow from one idea to the next in a logical, coherent manner. To do so successfully, you need to organize your content and employ a variety of writing strategies.

Content

Before you begin writing, you need to determine how you are going to organize the information you intend to present in your paper. This isn't just a matter of organizing your notes and time. At the very least, you need to review your purpose statement, be sure your paper aligns with it, and include evidence in support of any claims you make. The organizing pattern you select depends on what you hope to accomplish with your paper. Whatever pattern you select, however, should enable the reader to anticipate what to expect and provide a flow to your writing.

When deciding on a particular pattern, consider two key approaches: think about the sort of impression you want to create, and identify what will be gained by those reading what you've written. For example, how you organize your information and write a persuasive paper to get the reader to adopt a particular belief or action will be different from writing a how-to paper in which you describe how something is to be accomplished. The following are some of the more common organizing patterns:

Chronological: Presents a series of events in a sequence over a period of time

Pro/con: Arranges ideas to balance both sides of an argument or to favor one side over another

Descriptive: Describes a topic or subject in detail

Problem/solution: Defines a problem and discusses the appropriate solution(s)

Cause/effect: Discusses factors that lead to outcomes (e.g., cigarette smoking leads to lung cancer)

How-to: Explains how to do something or how something happens

Writing Strategies

In addition to the way you're going to write, you also need to think about how you're going to write. Success in this regard certainly depends on your command of the mechanics of writing, such as grammar and syntax. However, of equal or even greater significance is how you choose to incorporate and present information. To do so effectively, you will need to use a variety of writing techniques and strategies. The following are some general suggestions for organizing and presenting your content:

- Use a number of sources (i.e., don't rely too heavily on one source).
- Use a variety of sources of information (e.g., books, articles, interviews).
- Identify relevant evidence and incorporate it with each element you're offering in support of your thesis or purpose statement.
- Choose evidence that is consistent with the type of document you intend to write.
- Include an appropriate mix of personal information and perspectives as well as quotes and paraphrased material.

Focus on Quality

As noted earlier, the purpose of this chapter is not to provide a grammar lesson or to serve as a textbook on how to write. Too, research writing isn't exciting or meant to engage you like a mystery novel or best seller. It is purposely objective and is designed to present information that is accurate. Still, there are a variety of things you can do to improve the quality of your writing and enhance the overall readability of your paper.

Verb Variety

Reading the same verbs repeatedly tends to cause readers to overlook information or otherwise not read as closely as they might had different words been used. For example, when quoting other researchers, don't keep using "says." Use a thesaurus and come up with different ways of saying the same thing. Here, you might substitute words such as "notes" or "states" or related words such as "observes" or "suggests," depending on context. Even just using a different word every other time can change the tone of your paper considerably.

Transitions

Many beginning researchers mistakenly assume a term paper is simply a matter of gluing together various pieces of information they've acquired. They'll quote one person after another, often with little or no context. Not only is such writing difficult to read, it suggests you haven't learned anything or have nothing to contribute on the topic. Sometimes this is appropriate, as when you're trying to show that many researchers share the same point. Even so, you should try to incorporate intervening text that places the information in context, expresses your views on the matter, or sets the stage for information to follow.

Different Introductions

Similarly, when introducing someone else's material, don't just say, "Smith says." Try variation here as well. For example, you might try "In Smith's view," "According to Smith," or "Smith suggests." Generally, you will also refer to authors by only last name. For example, you would use "Walworth notes ..." and not "W. Walworth notes ..." or "Bill Walworth notes ...."

"Passed Tense"

Present tense is easy. Anything happening in the present should be discussed using the present tense. However, the same is true of information you discuss from people who have died. Your instructor may have suggestions. But, as a rule, use the historical present tense to present information in an active way from someone who has passed. For example, let's say you want to use a quote from Sigmund Freud. Instead of using "Freud said ...," you should use "Freud says ...."

Quotations

When incorporating quoted material in your paper, use variety in how you present it. There is no rule for how many quotations in a row is too many. But, too many quotes one after another will make your paper hard to read and even harder for the reader to put the content into context. Rather than including a series of successive quotes, break them up. Put some narrative text between each quotation or simply consider paraphrasing some.

On a related note, avoid quoting dictionaries. First of all, it's patronizing. Everyone has a dictionary to look up words. Second, citing a dictionary definition implies you don't know much about your own topic or otherwise don't know how to start your paper. Either way, many definitions are too vague or generalized to be useful. *If* you are going to use a dictionary, use one appropriate to the discipline of your topic. You might also find the word's definition in a professional, scholarly journal related to your topic.

Level

Write clearly, simply, and in a straightforward style. More importantly, write at a level that you're comfortable with and that you can both read and understand. Many students mistakenly assume that using highly technical, scholarly terms improves their work. However, trying to use material or terms you don't understand can do more damage than good. Be aware that using big words and jargon alone won't make your paper better. It will usually be quite clear to readers when you're using your words and when you're using someone else's. And whether you understand the terms you're using will be even more clear.

Format

Instructor- and assignment-specific formatting requirements aside (e.g., margins, font size), you need to think about how to visually present your information. Most word-processing software includes some sort of standard styles. These are designed to provide consistency throughout your document. For example, your headings may be in **bold** type or ALL CAPS, while your subheadings might be *italicized* or <u>underlined</u>. Whether you use a predefined set of styles or your own, you need to provide a consistent look and feel to your paper. Formatting such as abrupt font changes and varied line spacings are distracting, can be visually confusing, and can cause the reader to interpret your information incorrectly.

Charts can be particularly problematic in this respect. Very rarely will you find a chart with the information presented in the exact format you want. Rather than simply copying and pasting it into your paper, consider presenting the information in a different way. At the very least, think about retyping the chart using a font and other formatting that are consistent with the rest of your paper. If you include the chart as is, speak with your instructor to be sure you don't commit plagiarism. Conversely, if you remove information from the chart, decide whether what's left is best portrayed in a chart or whether presenting it in a narrative format might be stronger.

✔ TIPS

- Don't summarize one study after another.
- Don't remain uncritical. Include your views on the information you're using as well as your own views on the topic in general.
- Get feedback from others before submitting. Among other things, ask if they understand what you've written or if they have suggestions for improvement or for making your paper more readable.
- It can't be emphasized enough—as part of or in addition to the previous point, have someone proofread your work each time before you submit it.

Know When Enough Is Enough

It is difficult for many students to know when they're done writing. Some want to be done as quickly as possible, while others want to include more and more information. The right answer usually falls somewhere in between. Unfortunately, there is no easy answer that will apply to everyone for all assignments. However, there are a few signposts that can help you to know when you're done.

Check Your Assignment

First and foremost, make certain you've met or exceeded all your instructor's expectations for the assignment. The number of pages is certainly key. Not all professors will specify a number of pages. But, for those who do, be aware that the number typically reflects pages of content and not things like a title page or list of references. Likewise, if it's not clear, ask your instructor how partial pages will be treated. For example, if you're to write a ten-page paper but have only nine and a half pages of content, will the instructor round up from nine and a half to ten, or are you expected to come up with another half page of writing to meet the ten-page expectation?

Identify the Point of Diminishing Returns

More isn't necessarily better. Your writing should always be quality writing, and, at all costs, you should avoid including extra words or content just to meet some word or page number expectation. However, even with the best-written papers, there comes a point of diminishing returns. There is always going to be more information that you could include. And yet, if you have already discussed that information, it probably doesn't need to be mentioned again. Even if the information is new or somehow unique, if it doesn't add a new perspective or clarify a point noted elsewhere in your paper, it probably shouldn't be included.

Know the Difference between Writing and Editing

Pay attention to whether you're generating new content or merely editing what you've already written. If you're adding new points to your paper, continue. That's writing. But if you're merely changing one word to another or rewriting sentences or even entire passages, you're editing. This is not to say that editing isn't important. It is. You just need to acknowledge that you could edit forever if you don't make a conscious effort to stop. As noted, if the writing isn't adding a new perspective or making your points clearer, you should probably stop.

Protect Your Work

Because of the amount of time and effort involved, it is very tempting for some students to try to steal other students' work. For this and other reasons, you should never share your password(s) or data with another student. This includes not lending your paper to anyone or otherwise loading it on a public server or saving it on a machine that's readily accessible to others. If you find your work or file has been stolen, report it to your instructor immediately.

☑ TIPS

- On public workstations, save your work to a removable storage device or to a network storage location. Never save your work locally to a hard drive or to the desktop.
- Close your work—don't just save it—before removing your storage device. As a secondary precaution, exit the software and log off the machine (as appropriate).
- Save or print out all your files, rough drafts, and notes. Without such, you have no way of proving you wrote something.
- Make backup copies of your work regularly and frequently.

Be Your Own Advocate

Many students feel that asking their instructor for help or feedback will be seen as a sign of failure or ignorance on their part. Rather than risk raising a red flag about something they don't know or understand, such students decide to try to figure it out on their own. In reality, most professors are sympathetic to students seeking help and welcome, even encourage, questions. Again, compiling and writing a term paper poses a number of significant challenges. Especially if this is your first paper, having difficulty is not uncommon. Because it's expected, you shouldn't feel uncomfortable about asking questions or wanting feedback.

❓ REFLECTIONS

- Determine whether your institution has a writing center or similar services (e.g., tutors) where you can get help writing and editing your paper.

- Because you won't always be working on your own computer, determine whether the word-processing software you're using is compatible with that being used on your campus's computers. If not, learn how to save your paper in such a way that you can work on it on all the systems you're likely to use.

- Before starting to write, jot down the main ideas you're hoping to express. Then list smaller, related points for each. From there, you should be able to convert all this information into a working outline that you can then use as a framework for your writing.

- Review the skill sets discussed earlier in this chapter. Which ones are your strongest and which pose challenges to you? In what way(s)?

- Use the Focus on Quality elements discussed earlier in this chapter to review a rough draft of your paper. Which have you included and to what degree? How can you incorporate lesser used elements or even replace overused ones?

CHAPTER 13

Sample Search

· · · · · · · · · · · · · · · · · · · ·

Many techniques and strategies exist for conducting effective searches for information. Several of these are outlined throughout this book. Although there are many wrong ways to search for information, there is no single, right way. This chapter provides an overview of one specific strategy. As you seek information, you may choose to follow this strategy, adopt parts of it, or develop your own strategy altogether as you see fit.

Step 1: Select a Topic (see chapter 5)
· ·

Conscription is a process used to bolster enlistment in the military, particularly when there is a lack of sufficient volunteers. In the United States, conscription is more commonly known as *selective service* or even more informally as *the draft*. Many people, though, oppose the draft for religious, political, or other reasons. These individuals are known as *conscientious objectors*.

To avoid prosecution, many who opposed the draft fled to Canada and other countries during the 1960s. These individuals are often referred to as *draft dodgers*. Though many associate it with the Vietnam War, conscientious objection is not a new concept. For this example, we will focus on draft dodgers during the First World War.

Step 2: Generate a Purpose Statement (see chapter 5)
· ·

To find information on draft resisters during the First World War.

Step 3: Identify Possible
Initial Search Terms (see chapter 8)

Divide your terms into narrower, broader, related, and alternate categories. (*Note: You may not always be able to come up with a term that aligns 100 percent and may, instead, have to think broadly in terms of concepts.*)

	Draft Resisters	First World War
Related/Alternate	conscientious objection	World War One
	conscientious objectors	World War I
	draft dodgers	
	draft dodging	
Broader	military service	war
	selective service	
	conscription	
Narrower	peace movements	United States

Step 4: Identify Potential
Search Tools (see chapters 6 and 7)

The remainder of this chapter will focus on the following search tools.

- For books: PILOT (online library catalog)
- For articles: America: History and Life (AHL)
- For websites: Google (search engine)

Note, however, that these tools are only starting points and are being used for examples. Although most libraries have only one catalog, they are likely to have more than one search tool you can use to find articles and websites. Effective research requires a variety of search tools and resources.

The images that appear in this chapter reflect the configuration in place at Edinboro University of Pennsylvania at the time of writing. The availability, appearance, and functionality of resources depicted will differ at your institution and will change over time. Figure numbers correspond to the operational step being depicted. In instances where more than one point is being demonstrated, letters are used to clarify. For example, 13.2a refers to the first point associated with figure 13.2, 13.2b refers to the second point, and so on.

Step 5: Identify and Acquire Relevant Information Sources

In this step, you will begin searching for and acquiring possible sources of information on your topic using the tools listed in Step 4.

Books

1. On your library's home page, locate the link to your library's catalog. In this case, as shown in figure 13.1, the Library Catalog link (13.1a) accesses PILOT—the name of this library's online catalog.

FIGURE 13.1

Link Used to Access the Library Catalog of the Baron-Forness Library

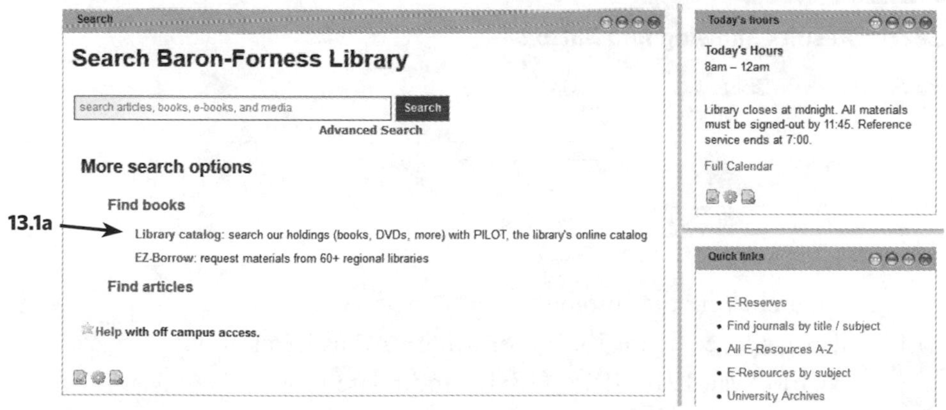

2. Selecting the link produces the default interface for the catalog (see figure 13.2), which in this case is Basic Search (13.2a). Enter one of the search terms you identified in Step 3. To conduct a search by subject, enter your terms in the Search For box (13.2b) and select "Subject Heading begins with . . ." from the drop-down menu to the right (13.2c). Figure 13.2 illustrates a search for books with "world war one" as a subject heading.

FIGURE 13.2

**Basic Search Interface with Initial "Subject Heading begins with . . ."
Search Entered**

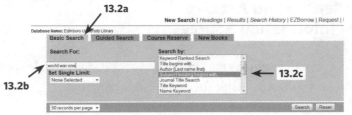

3. The search produces the screen shown in figure 13.3. At first glance, there do not appear to be any items with "world war one" as a subject. However, upon closer examination, there is an Info button (13.3a) associated with "World War One, 1914-1918."

FIGURE 13.3

Search Results Showing Info Button

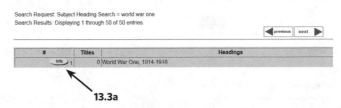

4. Upon clicking the Info button, a secondary set of results is displayed (see figure 13.4) indicating various items about "World War, 1914-1918" (13.4a) and related topics.

Partial List of Subject Headings Related to "World War, 1914-1918"

Search Request: Subject Heading Search = World War, 1914-1918   **13.4a**
Search Results: Displaying 1 through 50 of 50 entries.

◄ previous | next ►

#	Titles	Headings	Headings Type
[1]	142	World War, 1914-1918	Library of Congress subject headings
[2]	25	World War (1914-1918)	Faceted application of subject terminology
[3]	2	World War, 1914-1916	General Heading
[4]	1	World War, 1914-1918	LC Annotated Children's Catalog subject headings
[5]	13	World War, 1914-1918--Aerial operations	Library of Congress subject headings
[6]	2	World War, 1914-1918--Aerial operations, American	Library of Congress subject headings
[7]	3	World War, 1914-1918--Aerial operations, British	Library of Congress subject headings
[8]	1	World War, 1914-1918--Aerial operations, French	Library of Congress subject headings
[9]	2	World War, 1914-1918--Africa	Library of Congress subject headings
[10]	1	World War, 1914-1918--African American	Library of Congress subject headings
[11]	4	World War, 1914-1918--African Americans	Library of Congress subject headings
[12]	2	World War, 1914-1918--Anecdotes	Library of Congress subject headings
[13]	3	World War, 1914-1918--Arabian Peninsula	Library of Congress subject headings
[14]	1	World War, 1914-1918--Arabian Peninsula--Drama	Library of Congress subject headings
[15]	2	World War, 1914-1918--Armistices	Library of Congress subject headings
[16]	1	World War, 1914-1918--Armistices--Juvenile literature	Library of Congress subject headings

5. By clicking on the general "World War, 1914-1918" link, you are taken to a list of all 142 items in the collection with that as a subject heading (see figure 13.5). On the resultant list, check whether the item is available (13.5a). Also note the call number (13.5b) and location (13.5c) of items of interest. Note that the first three items on the list, as well as others, fall within the D521–D523 range (13.5d). If one of these items is useful, you could simply browse the shelves. That is, because similar subjects are shelved in the same general location, you might simply browse D520–D525 or so for other items on this topic.

Partial List of Items with "World War, 1914-1918" as a Subject Heading

Search Request: Subject Heading Search = world war, 1914-1918
Search Results: Displaying 1 through 50 of 142 entries.

◄ previous | next ►

13.5c   13.5b   **13.5a**

Sort Results by: [▼]   Post Limit

#	OPAC Subject Headings Search	Title	Author	Date
[1]	World War, 1914-1918	1914 / Lyn Macdonald.	Macdonald, Lyn	1988
	Library Location: Books -- Fourth Floor	Call Number: D521 .M23 1988	Status: Available	
[2]	World War, 1914-1918	American heritage history of World War I / by the editors of American heritage, the magazine of history. Narrative by S. L. A. Marshall; prologue by Edmund Stillman. Editor in charge: Alvin M. Josephy, Jr.; managing editor: Joseph L. Gardner.	Marshall, S. L. A. (Samuel Lyman Atwood), 1900-1977	1964
	Library Location: Books -- Fourth Floor	Call Number: D521 .M412	Status: Available	
[3]	World War, 1914-1918	Audacious war / by Clarence W. Barron.	Barron, Clarence W. (Clarence Walker), 1855-1928	1915
	Library Location: Books -- Fourth Floor	Call Number: D523 .B4	Status: Available	
[4]	World War, 1914-1918	Bath Day [electronic resource] / Looko Distribution GmbH.		2012
	Library Location: Online video	Call Number: *Electronic Resource	Status: Available	
[5]	World War, 1914-1918	Big Picture [electronic resource]: 42nd Rainbow Division / National Archives and Records Service.		2009
	Library Location: Online video	Call Number: *Electronic Resource	Status: Available	
[6]	World War, 1914-1918	Big Picture [electronic resource]: Army Medicine / National Archives and Records Service.		2009
	Library Location: Online video	Call Number: *Electronic Resource	Status: Available	
[7]	World War, 1914-1918	Bolshevism and world peace / introd. by Lincoln Steffens.	Trotsky, Leon, 1879-1940	1918
	Library Location: Books -- Fourth Floor	Call Number: D639.S8 T7 1918a	Status: Available	
[8]	World War, 1914-1918	Brief history of the great war.	Hayes, Carlton J. H. (Carlton Joseph Huntley), 1882-1964	1920
	Library Location: Books -- Fourth Floor	Call Number: D521 .H35	Status: Available	
[9]	World War, 1914-1918	Central Europe / a translation by Christabel M. Meredith from the original German of Mittel-Europa.	Naumann, Friedrich, 1860-1919	1971
	Library Location: Books -- Fourth Floor	Call Number: D443 .N4 1971	Status: Available	
[10]	World War, 1914-1918	Christ or Mars? / by Will Irwin.	Irwin, Will, 1873-1948	1923
	Library Location: Books -- Fourth Floor	Call Number: D523 .I6	Status: Available	

13.5d

6. Now, you could select and examine one of the items from the list in figure 13.5 for more information and ideas for additional search strategies. For example, figure 13.6 shows the complete record for the first item on the list—Macdonald's book *1914*. By looking at the Subject(s) field, you can see "World War, 1914-1918" listed (13.6a), indicating this is a general book on the topic. But the field also lists "World War, 1914-1918 Causes" (13.6b), which means the book discusses causes of the war as a primary subject as well. If you wanted other items on this subject, you could simply click on the link.

FIGURE 13.6

Complete Record for First Item from Results List

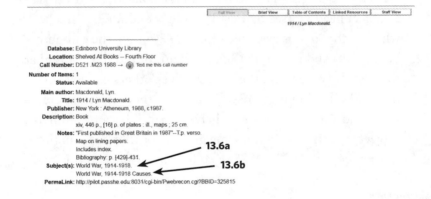

Clearly there are hundreds of books on this subject. So, why weren't any results produced by the search for "world war one" as a subject? Remember, terms used in subject heading searches have to match approved subject headings *exactly*. In this case, the word *one* is not part of the accepted subject heading for this topic. Instead, the approved heading is "world war, 1914-1918." One way to address this problem is to do a keyword search for your terms. Then examine a few records of titles that seem promising and click on one or more relevant subject headings to find similar books on your topic.

7. Guided Search: If you refer to your initial search (see Books, step 2), you'll recall you began with a Basic Search. However, this search tool also has a Guided Search tab. You might want to try this search option in order to be certain you've searched as thoroughly as possible or as an alternate search strategy. Upon selecting Guided Search (13.7a), you are taken to the screen shown in figure 13.7. It presents your search options in a different way. For example, using the first drop-down menu (Search for), you can ask to search "any of your terms," "all of your terms," or your terms "as a phrase." The default is "all of these" (13.7b). You can use the second drop-down menu—Search In—to indicate where the terms should appear. In this case, Keyword Anywhere is the default (13.7c).

FIGURE 13.7

Guided Search Interface

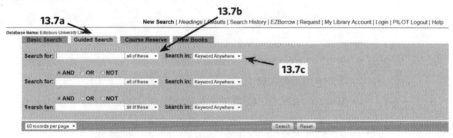

Articles

1. For articles, just as you did for books, you need to select an appropriate search tool. If you look back to figure 13.1 (see Books, step 1), you'll notice a Find Articles link on the library's home page. Although this is a logical starting point, the All E-Resources A-Z link (in the Quick links box) is the most comprehensive and, therefore, a better place to begin, as you may discover nonarticle sorts of search tools you might use. Figure 13.8 shows the initial portion of the screen that results by selecting the All E-Resources A-Z link.

FIGURE 13.8

Partial Alphabetized Listing of Available Electronic Search Tools

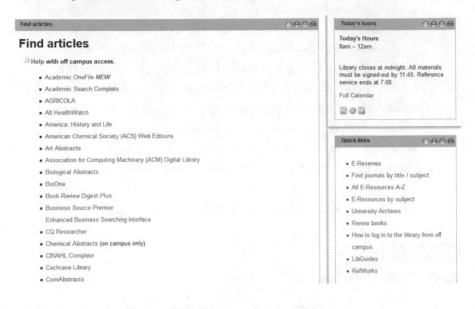

2. On this list of search tools, which can be used to find articles and other information (e.g., book reviews), two immediately seem like they might be relevant to your search.

> Academic Search Complete: This search tool is an inch deep and a mile wide. That means it is a good starting point because it covers a lot of topics in general but none in much detail.

> America: History and Life (AHL): As suggested by the title, this search tool is a good one to use to find information on American history and life. Because it covers a very specific topic in a lot of detail, it is an inch wide and a mile deep. For its depth of coverage and focus, select this search tool. Figure 13.9 shows the opening screen for AHL.

FIGURE 13.9

Opening Screen for America: History and Life

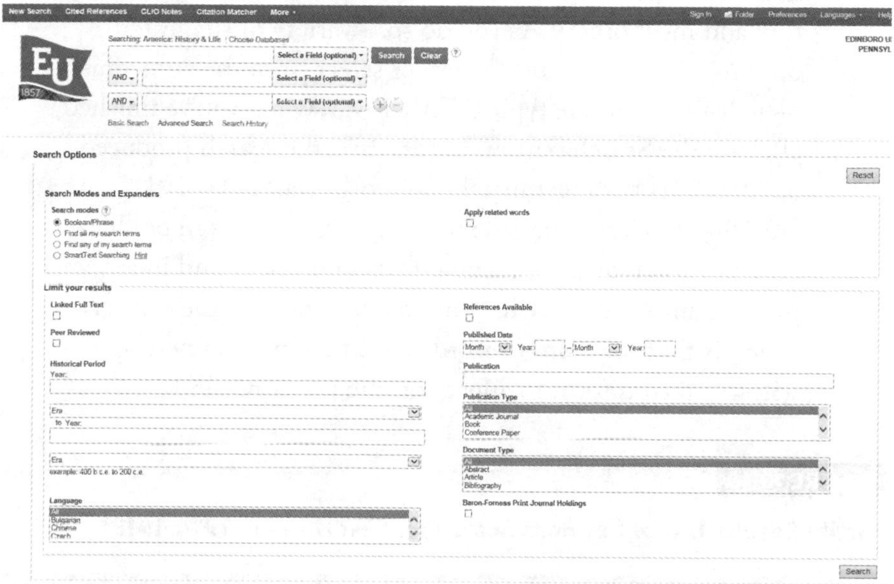

Because every resource is different and because interfaces change frequently, it is impossible to generate and discuss a search strategy that will work every time with every search tool. This is especially true of search tools used to find articles. As you become familiar with searching, you will develop your own style. This chapter follows one suggested method and uses the Search History option. Not all resources have this option. But, for those that do, it enables you to see at a glance which searches are working and which are not. You can then mix, match, and revise your searches quickly and easily.

3. Because it worked for finding books, begin by entering "world war, 1914-1918" (see figure 13.10). Conduct the search as a keyword search (13.10a)—the default search for this search tool and most others. As you do so, a variety of suggested options will appear. You can either select from the autocomplete list or continue typing. Either way, when you've finished, click on the Search button. In this case, the search produced 5,040 results with text matching "world war, 1914-1918" (13.10b). Be aware that all matching text appears in boldface (13.10c) and that the matching text might be found in any place in any order anywhere in an item's record. The only criterion is that the word or words have to appear somewhere within a record for it to appear on the list of results.

FIGURE 13.10

Partial Results List of Keyword Search for "World War, 1914-1918"

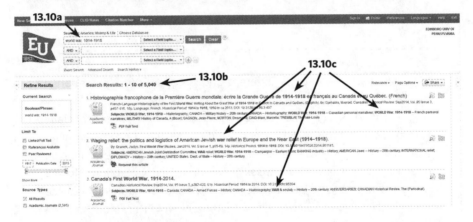

4. Next, look at the citation information and identify possible subject terms that correspond to your topic. Clicking on the title of an article that looks as though it might be useful provides the complete record (figure 13.11). In this case, similar to what you experienced when finding books, the item record shows "World War, 1914-1918" as a subject heading (13.11a).

FIGURE 13.11

Record Showing Hyperlinked "World War, 1914-1918" in Subject Terms Field

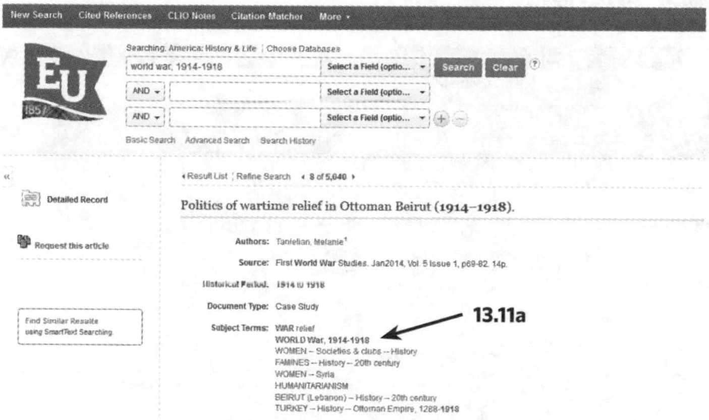

13.11a

5. Similar to a search for books, clicking on "World War, 1914-1918" in the list of subject terms will produce a list of results with that term as the subject heading (figure 13.12). Note that the term is inserted into the search box surrounded by quotation marks and with DE at the beginning (13.12a). The quotation marks indicate that the term is to be searched as a phrase, with the words in the order in which they appear in the search box. DE is just a code for *DEscriptor*, used in this search tool to indicate that it is searching all descriptors containing "world war, 1914-1918." That is, this search tool will find "world war, 1914-1918" as well as more specific topical areas, such as "world war, 1914-1918—Canada" and "world war, 1914-1918—campaigns." Notice that searching this way significantly focuses your results—from 5,040 to 3,910 (13.12b).

Partial Results List Obtained from Subject Field Search for "World War, 1914-1918"

13.12a

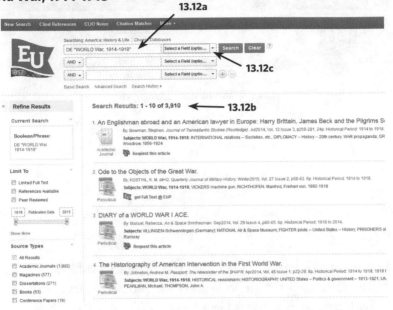

If you were to click on the drop-down menu (13.12c), you would find a list of other codes and their associated fields (e.g., TI for Title, AU for author) that are used in this search tool. These codes and how they're displayed will vary from resource to resource but are a quick and easy way to focus your search—assuming you know the correct term(s) to use.

6. It is now time to look for information on the other half of your purpose statement: draft resisters. Based on your search for books and on what you just discovered while searching for articles, "World War, 1914-1918" appears to be a standard subject heading. It is unclear if the same is true for "draft resisters." Therefore, begin by conducting a new key-

word search using "draft resisters." From the resultant list, browse through the subject headings of several records to find a match to "draft resisters" or other, alternate headings you might use. After doing so, some that appear relevant are these:

draft resisters	conscientious objectors	conscientious objection—history
pacifism	conscientious objection	draft—United States—history
Mennonites	war—religious aspects	peace movements—United States

Because you originally searched for "draft resisters" and because that term appears as a specific subject heading in at least one of the records, open that record and click on the heading "DRAFT resisters." Now look at figure 13.13. First, notice that DE is inserted as the field code (13.13a) just as it was in the preceding search. Again, this is a two-letter abbreviation indicating that the search tool is looking for all descriptors (DE) that might include "draft resisters." Don't worry. This is just something this search tool does. It is actually a very good thing in that the search is slightly broader in scope than a specific subject search. As also happened earlier, the results set is more limited—70 items versus 89 (13.13b). The smaller number could be because this search is finding all records with both words in the subject field versus finding text that matches "draft" or "resisters" (i.e., via keyword searching). Or, it could simply be that there aren't many items with "draft resisters" as a subject heading. At this point, because of the relatively small number of results, you may wish to use the results generated from this heading or try one of the others identified earlier.

FIGURE 13.13

**Partial Results List Obtained by Clicking on the Subject Heading
"DRAFT Resisters"**

13.13a

13.13b

7. Having conducted subject searches on the main parts of your purpose statement, it is now time to begin focusing your results by combining your searches (see figure 13.14). To do this, click on the Search History link beneath the search boxes (13.14a). Upon doing so, you will see a table listing each of your four searches so far (13.14b)—two keyword and two DE/subject searches. Note that the table also shows any limits (13.14c) you may have placed on your searches, such as date range or publication level (in this example, no limits were incorporated), and the number of items each search generated (13.14d).

FIGURE 13.14

Search History Link and Search History

13.14a

13.14c

13.14d

13.14b

8. Figure 13.15 illustrates how to combine multiple searches. As your two best, most specific searches are 2 and 4, simply click the box in front of each search—S2 and S4, respectively (13.15a)—and then click Search with AND (13.15b) to combine both searches. This will produce results containing *both* "world war, 1914-1918" and "draft resisters" as subject headings. This is a much more focused, narrower search than simply finding matching text somewhere in an item's record (i.e., a keyword search).

FIGURE 13.15

Combining Searches 2 (S2) and 4 (S4) Using the Search with AND Button

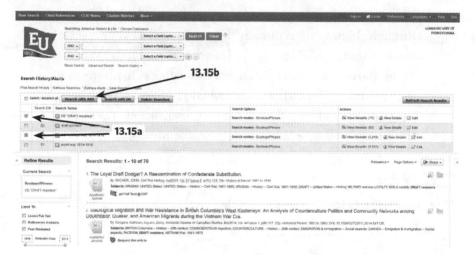

9. Figure 13.16 shows how the preceding combined search (13.16a) results in five articles matching your search criteria (13.16b).

Results (Five Items) of Combining Searches 2 (S2) and 4 (S4)

10. You now need to get the actual articles so you can read through them to determine if they are useful to your research needs. Figure 13.17 shows the four access methods available at this particular library. These are indicated at the bottom of each record (13.17a–d) and described in table 13.1. Although the wording will be different for your institution's resources, the articles will be available via the same means.

Different Methods for Accessing Articles

TABLE 13.1

Options for Acquiring Articles Using the AHL Search Tool at EUP

HTML Full Text (13.17a)	Text is directly available and optimized for display in a web browser
	Lacks formatting (e.g., pagination, fonts) found in printed article
	Images present in printed article may not be included
	Easy to copy/paste and otherwise manipulate text
	Hyperlinks enable navigation among the article's elements
	Generally cited differently than printed or PDF version
PDF Full Text (13.17b)	Text is directly available and is an exact, electronic copy of the original
	Image-based—an exact, electronic copy of the original with all the formatting, pagination, images, and so on
	Generally cited the same as printed version
get Full Text @ EUP (13.17c)	May link to another resource containing the electronic version or may direct you to a physical copy available in the library or both
Request this article (13.17d)	The article is not available in either electronic or physical format and must be requested from another library via interlibrary loan (ILL)

11. For linked items, you may or may not be taken directly to the article. For some articles, you will be taken to another search tool that provides access to the article; for others, you may be taken to an external site or search tool. Sometimes you may be taken only to the volume or even just to the title, at which point you will need to supply additional information (e.g., date, page numbers) to gain access to the article. When directed to other search tools and sites, you may find it helpful to conduct a search there (when possible) for additional information. That is, if an article you want is found there, perhaps there will be other sources of information you can use.

If you look back at figure 13.9, when you began your search for articles, you could have simply entered each term in its own Search box, clicked Subject Heading from the drop-down menu, and generated the same set of five results. However, if you mistyped or misspelled anything or if you didn't enter the *exact* subject heading, you probably would have retrieved few, if any, citations. Worse, you wouldn't have been able to isolate what went wrong (or right) with your search strategy. Although it may seem more tedious, Search History is a great way for beginning researchers to see at a glance not only what was entered but also what's working and what's not.

Reminders

It is rare that any single term or strategy will find all the information you need on your topic. Although they are certainly a good starting point in your research, the five articles identified in the preceding search may not be exactly what you want or all that you need. Keep in mind that they represent only the articles that had both "world war, 1914-1918" and "draft resisters" as subjects. That is, they are the only ones that matched your search criteria. So, although the following guidelines have already been mentioned, it is important to make note of some things you can do at this point to broaden or narrow your search for books and articles.

1. *Impose or remove limits to narrow or broaden your search.* Sometimes you may need to set a limit as part of your overall search. Maybe you want to limit your search to academic journals or to articles published within the past five years. However, setting limits early may unnecessarily restrict your search. Many students, for example, set their initial searches to retrieve only full-text. This has the advantage of producing only articles that are directly available electronically. But it may eliminate articles available electronically via other search tools. It will certainly eliminate those available in printed format within the library. As a result, you may have to spend more time looking for something you can use when an equally helpful source may be just a few clicks or steps away.

2. *Try alternate terms* (see Step 3 and Articles, step 5). Though not exactly the same thing, you might try "conscientious objectors" or "draft dodgers" instead of "draft resisters."

3. *Try broader, narrower, or related terms and concepts* (see Step 3). There may not be a book or article on exactly what you are researching. Sometimes you may have to find a source that deals with your topic more generally and then look for information you can use or parallels you can make to your specific topic. For example, here you might try the concept of "pacifism" (the practice of peace or nonviolence) or "Mennonites" (a group historically known for opposing war and violence).

4. *Alter your search strategy.* There are many different types of searches you can and should try. Among others, try mixing and matching and otherwise combining keyword and subject searches. Search for other books and articles by the same author. Add or remove a search limit. Examine your list of journals for commonalities and simply browse other issues.

5. *Change search tools.* Many of the preceding strategies apply to search tools as well. For example, if you did not find what you wanted in America: History and Life, try a more general search tool. Conversely, if you found too much information, try a search tool dealing with a specific aspect of your topic, such as political or religious reasons for conscientious objection.

6. *Change topics.* This should be your last resort and become an option only after you have spoken with *both* your instructor and a librarian. Especially for beginning researchers, many times the problem isn't that there's not enough information on a given topic, it is merely that the student doesn't know how to find and acquire it.

7. *Ask for help!* This cannot be emphasized enough. Admittedly, everyone gets stuck at some point (or multiple points) in the research process. However, do not waste countless hours

floundering without getting results. Getting a simple tip or two is often all it takes to get things rolling.

Websites

As with searching for books and articles, there are all sorts of search engines you can use to search the Web for information. Moreover, the search engine of choice today may not be so in the future. Currently, Google is arguably the predominant search engine of choice and has been used to construct the examples that follow.

1. Access Google (google.com).

2. Figure 13.18 shows the opening screen of the Internet search engine Google. At this point, you could simply type in a search by entering keywords in the search box (13.18a). On the day of this search, entering "world war, 1914-1918 draft resisters" produced more than 119,000 records. Obviously, this is not a very sophisticated or focused search. Instead, if you click on Settings in the lower right-hand corner, a pop-up menu appears. Selecting Advanced Search (13.18b) will present you with a variety of additional search options.

FIGURE 13.18

Default Google Search Screen Showing Advanced Search Option

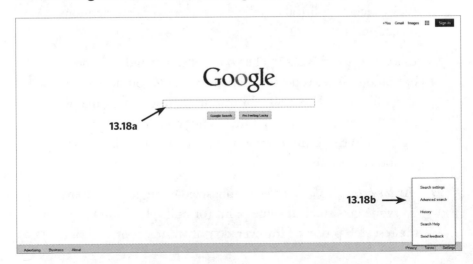

3. Figure 13.19 shows the default screen for Google's Advanced Search option. Note that the Advanced Search screen provides a number of additional search options to assist you in better focusing your results. Brief explanatory notes appear to the right of each option.

FIGURE 13.19

Google's Default Advanced Search Screen

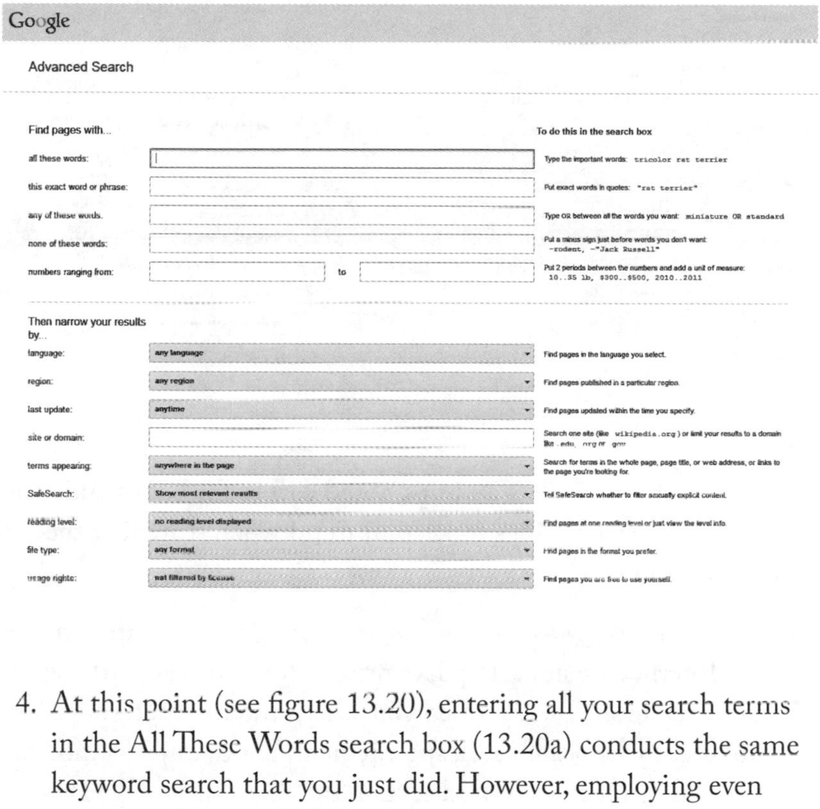

4. At this point (see figure 13.20), entering all your search terms in the All These Words search box (13.20a) conducts the same keyword search that you just did. However, employing even just one of the available limits can quickly narrow your search to a much more manageable number. At the very least, you should select a language (13.20b). The best information in the world will not be any good to you if you cannot read it. So, as a starting point, from the drop-down menu, select the language you are able to read best (e.g., English).

FIGURE 13.20

Advanced Google Keyword Search with Language Limit Selected

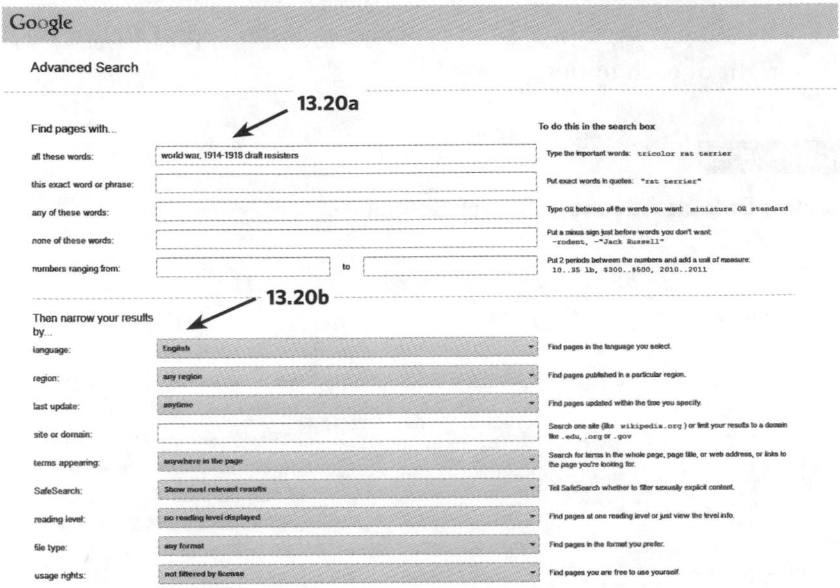

Reminders

In addition to the reminders and tips noted earlier for books and articles, there are a few specific things to keep in mind when searching the Internet for information.

1. *Remember that Internet searching is by keyword only.* Sites on the Internet are not set up like records for books and articles in search tools. That is, when you search the Internet, you cannot focus your search on a specific field. For example, although you can conduct a keyword search for "Shakespeare," you cannot limit your search to the subject of "Shakespeare" or to books written by him. The best you can do is to find sites containing the word "Shakespeare." This explains why a search often produces as many good sites as bad.

2. *Learn how your search engine generates and displays results.* Every search engine has its own unique way of ranking results—the

way sites are listed on the results screen. What appears high on one search engine's results list may appear lower on another's. Always read through at least one to two screens of results for relevant information. If you are still not finding relevant sites, read through the search engine's About or Help features to learn how results are ranked and appear.

3. *Impose additional limits on your search.* To help remedy the preceding problems, consider placing one or more additional limits on your search. For example, one common choice is to select "in the title of the page" under the Terms Appearing option. As the heading suggests, this will produce only sites with your words in the title of the page. Other common limits you might consider using include Last Update and Reading Level.

4. *Beware of sponsored links.* Many links often appear in and around your actual results. These are called *sponsored links* and are essentially advertisements. They appear because they are related to your search, page content, or both. However, they typically have little, if any, value to your research and should generally be ignored.

5. *Try Google Scholar (http://scholar.google.com).* Google Scholar is a search engine designed specifically to search for scholarly literature. Because of such, it has its own unique set of search options. In addition, many academic libraries link their search tools to Google Scholar. For example, if you search for a particular book via Google Scholar, there may be a link to your library's catalog from which you can locate and retrieve the book.

6. *Try another search engine.* If you are confident you have entered a good search but still are not getting the results you want, consider changing to a different search engine. Again, every search engine has different search features and options. You need to find the right tool that will produce the information you are seeking.

7. *Remember that the Internet is just a tool.* For reasons addressed earlier, few instructors will allow you to use only websites in your research. Even so, though the Internet admittedly provides access to an overwhelming abundance of information, it is important to remember that not everything can be found or is available on the Internet. The most effective research will combine information from books, articles, *and* websites.

Next Steps

Having acquired an initial set of some potentially useful sources of information, it is now time to begin reading, evaluating each source against the others. By doing so, you will find the sources that align best with your information needs. For all your sources, but especially for those sources you find more relevant than others, jot down the main idea(s) and take notes on key points, terms, and concepts. These can be used to generate additional searches should you need more information. And be sure to write down the complete citation information for all the sources you decide to use.

A Final Reminder

At this point, once they have found the required number of sources, many beginning researchers breathe a sigh of relief, mistakenly believing that they are done having to search for information. However, as has been noted several times, research is a process. Conducting a single, perfect search that yields exactly what you want the first time is possible but highly unlikely.

In addition, as you begin reading through your sources more closely, two things will occur. First, you will find that some of the sources you've acquired aren't as relevant as they might at first have seemed. Some of the sources simply may not have as *much* of or the *kind* of information you are seeking. In fact, some might not even be appropriate at all.

Second, and not surprisingly, you will learn new information as you read. After all, isn't that why you're doing the research in the first place? But what you learn won't necessarily be limited solely to content. You'll also gain new insights and perspectives on your topic. In turn, this may generate new areas of interest you may wish to explore within your topic.

What does this mean to your research and your paper? Using the topic outlined in this chapter, let's say, for example, that you need to find ten articles and have decided you want to focus on American draft resisters. As you read through two of your articles, you discover they're more about the French and have very little to do with Americans. What should you do?

- **Option 1: The Easy Thing**—The *easy* thing to do is simply to settle and somehow find a way to use the two sources. Admittedly, you could incorporate a single quote from each and thereby meet the assignment requirement to use ten articles. However, that you've done so will usually be pretty obvious from the instructor's side of the desk. Such information stands out and can be confusing in that it has little, if anything, to do with your topic. It also suggests you're being lazy or simply don't care. Either way, the quality of your writing and the quality of your overall paper are likely to suffer as a consequence.

- **Option 2: The Right Thing**—If you want to do the *right* thing, here are two approaches.

  ▸ *Modify your topic.* Just because the articles don't align well with your topic doesn't mean they contain bad information. They're just not as relevant as you'd like them to be. But this doesn't mean you need to change your topic and start over. Rather, modify your topic slightly to be able to incorporate the new, divergent information. In the sample search, for example, instead of inserting some random quote that has no bearing on your topic, you could broaden your topic to "World War I draft resisters from around the world" (not just the United States). It would then be perfectly reasonable to incorporate the two articles by drawing comparisons between French and American draft resisters.

  ▸ *Search for additional information.* Most students don't want to hear this. But, if you really want to stay with your initial topic, the best thing to do is simply to discard the two articles and try to find two that are more aligned with your topic. To do so, you could re-create some of your earlier searches or you might construct a new search strategy using some of the terms and concepts you've compiled through your reading and research efforts so far.

Which of these two options you choose is entirely up to you. Either way, always remember that finding the information you want involves the coordination of separate but related steps. Also keep in mind that good research is a matter of searching and searching again—literally *re*searching—using different terms, strategies, and tools. As with any endeavor, the more research you do, the easier it becomes. But there aren't any shortcuts. To conduct effective and efficient research requires time, practice, and patience. When you find yourself struggling—and at some point you will—ask for help to discover why your searches haven't been successful and, more importantly, to learn what you can do to make them successful.

GLOSSARY

You will hear or otherwise encounter many terms throughout your research experience. It is beyond the scope of this book to provide a complete, exhaustive list of such. What follows is a summary of the key concepts, terms, and ideas mentioned in this book that you'll need to understand in order to successfully navigate through the research process.

abstract. A summary providing an overview of key points, issues, findings, conclusions, and other information presented in your paper.

academic library. Supports the curriculum, research, teaching, and information needs of a college or university. Larger institutions may have multiple libraries, each geared toward meeting a specific information or institutional need (e.g., social sciences, general undergraduate). Compare to **public library, school library, special library**.

academic publications. See **scholarly publications**.

accuracy. A concept used in evaluating information that refers to the degree to which the information is correct. Compare to **readability, relevancy**.

all-nighter. An informal term referring to staying up all night to complete a project; often stated as "pulling an all-nighter."

almanac. A publication providing data, tables, figures, statistics, and other information on a variety of topics and subjects.

appendix (pl. appendices). Placed at the end of your paper, an appendix provides greater detail about a topic discussed in your paper. For example, whereas you might discuss a policy in your paper, the full text of the policy might be included at the end as an appendix.

argumentative/opinion paper. A type of term paper in which you take a stand on a topic and justify it with evidence—either for or against. Both sides—pro and con—of the issue are typically discussed. Compare to **descriptive/informative paper, compare/contrast paper**.

authentication. The procedure used to access a given search tool or information resource. Typically the login requires a username and password that recognize you as an authorized, or authentic, user.

bias. A perspective taken on a topic.

bibliographic instruction. See **instruction**.

bibliography. 1. A list of sources used to write, and cited in, a paper. Also called *reference page, source list, works cited.* 2. A list of sources on a given topic.

body. The major part of a term paper in which you cite and use experts' opinions to provide evidence in support of your purpose and to answer your research questions.

Boolean operator. Also called *logical operator.* A word or symbol used to make a logical connection between two or more search terms. Common Boolean operators include AND, OR, and NOT.

brainstorming. A variety of techniques in which you write down as much as possible without any sort of editing or analysis. Once your list is complete, you then look for patterns, relationships, and other insights into what you've written.

capstone paper. See **term paper**.

catalog. Also called *OPAC, online public access catalog.* A type of search tool typically associated with locating information, particularly within a given library or location. An OPAC, for example, is a searchable catalog of the books, journals, and other items held by a library.

circ. See **circulation desk**.

circ desk. See **circulation desk**.

circulation. See **circulation desk**.

circulation desk. Also called *circ, circ desk, circulation.* The location (usually at or near the library's entrance) where you check out, return, and renew library materials, pay fines, and get general information. Compare to **reference desk**.

citation. A technique for properly attributing information to the appropriate author or source.

citation style. A prescribed set of stylistic and formatting conventions for citing sources in a consistent manner within a given discipline. APA (American Psychological Association) style, for example, is used by the social sciences. Differences among styles revolve around what information is required, how it's to be formatted, and where it's to be placed.

citation style manual. Also called *style guide*, *style manual*. An owner's manual of sorts, detailing the specific formatting and style conventions for a given citation style.

citing. See **citation**.

clustering. A brainstorming technique in which you write down random words, concepts, names, and so on associated with your topic. When you've finished, you impose order by circling related terms, color-coding, using arrows or lines, and similar techniques. Compare to **cubing**, **freewriting**.

compare/contrast paper. A type of term paper used to compare and contrast one topic, theme, idea—just about anything—with another by describing similarities and differences relative to the thesis. Compare to **argumentative/opinion paper**, **descriptive/informative paper**.

conclusion. The part of your term paper where you reflect on key points you've made, synthesizing and otherwise pulling together all the information you've presented in the body of your work in reference to your research questions and overall purpose statement.

controlled vocabulary. A standardized set of words used by a search tool to help ensure that similar information is indexed and searchable in the same way.

critical reading. Reading material for both relevance and accuracy by critically comparing and contrasting other items you have read or experienced as well as examining the historical, cultural, and other contexts of the information to better understand it. Compare to **skimming**.

cubing. A brainstorming technique in which you examine your topic from six different perspectives, or sides of a cube. Common perspectives include *describe*, *compare*, *associate*, *analyze*, *apply*, and *argue for* (or *against*). Once you've completed your cube, you look for relationships. Compare to **clustering**, **freewriting**.

database. An organized, searchable collection of stored data. Compare to **index**.

deadline. Also called *due date*. The date an assignment or part of an assignment is due to be completed and submitted.

descriptive/informative paper. A type of term paper that describes the nature of a topic, allowing you to acquire a deeper knowledge of the subject or issue. You may or may not be expected to discuss your own feelings and beliefs. Compare to **argumentative/opinion paper, compare/contrast paper**.

dictionary. A listing of words, terms, and concepts and their definitions, often with pronunciations. Dictionaries can be general or may be specific to a discipline or topic. A dictionary of psychology, for example, would focus on psychological terms and concepts.

due date. See **deadline**.

electronic full-text. See **full-text**.

encyclopedia. A book or multivolume set of books with essays covering a variety of topics in general or specific subjects in more detail. An encyclopedia of World War II, for example, would provide an overview of a variety of topics related to this war.

endnote. Acknowledges the work of another in the text of your narrative through the use of a superscripted number that is then referenced at the end of the chapter, section, or work. For example, "Abcde[1]" would correspond to endnote 1 at the end of your paper. Compare to **footnote, in-text citation**.

fallacy. An error in reasoning that eliminates or diminishes the accuracy of information. Fallacies can occur intentionally or unintentionally.

field. Used to store specific information in a specific location within a record. Compare to **database, index, record**.

field search. Enables you to search through a database by focusing on words contained in a specific field within a record. A search of the author field for "Shakespeare," for example, would retrieve item records in which "Shakespeare" appears in the author field. Compare to **keyword search**.

filters. See **search limits**.

final draft. The final version of your document that you submit to your instructor. Compare to **rough draft**.

footnote. Acknowledges the work of another in the text of your narrative through the use of a superscripted number that is then referenced at the bottom of the page. For example, "Abcde[1]" would correspond to footnote 1 at the bottom of the page on which the reference occurs. Compare to **endnote, in-text citation**.

freewriting. A brainstorming technique in which you write down anything and everything that comes to mind. Because you're likely to discover themes and insights you hadn't considered before, this is an excellent strategy for developing your topic. Compare to **clustering, cubing**.

full-text. Also called *electronic full-text.* Typically refers to the printed version of an article converted to electronic format that can be viewed, downloaded, and printed directly.

Google Scholar. A web search tool focusing on scholarly content.

hypothesis. Reflects a perspective you have on your thesis and what you believe your research will reveal.

ILL. See **interlibrary loan**.

index. Points to where information (e.g., articles, books) can be found. Many search tools are often referred to as indexes because they point researchers to articles and other types of content on a topic. Compare to **database**.

information desk. See **reference desk**.

inherent value. Refers to the relative significance attached to a particular part of your grade. For example, the research element may be 75 percent of your grade while the writing and grammar portion is 25 percent. In this case, clearly the instructor is placing more inherent value on the research portion. Compare to **relative value**.

instruction. Also called *bibliographic instruction, library instruction, user education.* Provided by librarians to teach users how to access and use library and other information resources and services more effectively and more efficiently.

intellectual property. Refers to property created through the use of the mind (i.e., intellect), encompassing a wide variety of original creations, including manuscripts, recordings, artwork, inventions, performances, and designs. See also **plagiarism**.

intentional plagiarism. Deliberate stealing of another's ideas or representing such as your own. See also **plagiarism, unintentional plagiarism, self-recycling**.

interface. The graphic representation or display of the features within a particular search tool or piece of software.

interlibrary loan (ILL). A service enabling you to acquire books and articles from other libraries when your library doesn't provide direct access to such.

in-text citation. Acknowledges the work of another in the text of your narrative. For example, (Smith, 2014) at the end of a sentence means that it originated from the source in your bibliography attributed to Smith and published in the year 2014. Compare to **footnote, endnote**.

introduction. The part of a term paper that expresses why the paper is being written, how the topic is being approached, and what appropriate key points are being presented.

keyword search. Searches an entire item record for text matching the keywords you've entered. Words may appear side by side or in reverse order and be separated by other words. Compare to **field search**.

LCSH. See **Library of Congress Subject Headings**; see also **controlled vocabulary**.

librarian. A professional trained in storing, accessing, and using information. Many librarians have specific areas of subject expertise (e.g., literature, chemistry), specialize in one aspect of librarianship (e.g., instruction), and have multiple responsibilities (e.g., reference and electronic resource management) within the library.

library. An organized, accessible collection of information that can be physical or virtual or both in nature.

library instruction. See **instruction**.

Library of Congress Subject Headings (LCSH). A commonly used controlled vocabulary of subject terms used by many librarians to organize items within their collections. See also **controlled vocabulary**.

limiters. See **search limits**.

limits. See **search limits**.

logical operator. See **Boolean operator**.

mapping. See **clustering**.

microcard. A type of microform in which content is stored on opaque sheets, requiring a special viewer to read, print, or download. Compare to **microfilm, microfiche, ultrafiche**; see also **microforms**.

microfiche. A type of microform in which content is stored on small, rectangular, transparent plastic sheets, requiring a special viewer to read, print, or download. Compare to **microfilm, ultrafiche, microcard**; see also **microforms**.

microfilm. A type of microform in which content is stored on long rolls of transparent film. Compare to **microcard, microfiche, ultrafiche**; see also **microforms**.

microforms. Storage mediums on which reduced-scale books, periodicals, and monographs are published. Because the reduction is so significant, microforms require a special reader to magnify, download, or print content. Microforms include **microfilm, microcard, microfiche,** and **ultrafiche**.

monograph. A publication that is produced only once and that typically covers a single subject, topic, or person in great detail. Compare to **periodical**.

online public access catalog. See **catalog**.

OPAC. See **catalog**.

paper mill. See **term paper mill**.

paraphrasing. A means of incorporating text into your paper using roughly the same amount of words as the original but restating the information without quoting it. Compare to **summarizing, quoting**.

peer-reviewed publications. Also called *refereed publications*. Publications in which the content is *very* focused and is reviewed by a group of peers "in the know" before it is published. As a result, information contained in these publications is seen as being of the highest caliber. All peer-reviewed publications are scholarly, but not all scholarly publications are peer-reviewed. Compare to **scholarly publications, popular publications**.

periodical. A publication that is produced regularly. Magazines and newspapers are examples. Compare to **monograph**.

phrase searching. A type of search used for multiple words in a specific order, such as *social security* or *national football league*. Quotation marks and parentheses are common ways to group words together as a phrase (e.g., "social security").

plagiarism. Inadvertent or purposeful stealing of intellectual property by failing to properly acknowledge the owner. See also **intellectual property**.

popular publications. Publications in which the content is both written and presented in a way intended to be understood by the public and individuals with little to no expertise with or knowledge about the subject being discussed. Compare to **scholarly publications, peer-reviewed publications**.

primary research. Firsthand, original research for which you are the individual conducting and reporting on the actual experiment or topic of the research and seeking to answer a specific question or set of related questions. Various methods such as experiments, surveys, and interviews are used to collect data. An experiment in which you attempt to determine the effectiveness of drug X in curing autism would be an example of primary research. Compare to **secondary research**.

primary source. Medium for presenting primary research. Examples include scholarly communications such as peer-reviewed articles, conference presentations, and lectures. Speeches, diaries, interviews, live performances, original reports, autobiographies, and eyewitness accounts and observations are also considered primary sources. Compare to **secondary source**.

proofreading. The process of reviewing a written document to identify grammar errors, misspellings, stylistic concerns (e.g., word choice), and other editorial shortcomings.

public library. Serves the community in which it is located, with an emphasis on leisure reading (e.g., best sellers) and other items of interest to the general population (e.g., self-help books). Many have specialized departments that focus on a specific population or service, such as children or genealogy. Compare to **academic library, school library, special library**.

purpose statement. See **thesis statement**.

quoting. A means of incorporating text into your paper using the exact wording and formatting of the original. Compare to **summarizing, paraphrasing**.

readability. A concept used in evaluating information that refers to how easily a source can be read. Compare to **accuracy, relevancy**.

record. A single document stored in a database, or a citation in an index. Compare to **database, field, index**.

refereed publications. See **peer-reviewed publications**.

reference. A service to address your information needs. See also **reference desk, reference librarian**; compare to **virtual reference**.

reference desk. Also called *information desk*. Staffed by reference librarians, this is the place to go in the library when you're seeking help with choosing a topic, selecting resources, and other aspects of your research assignment. Most libraries also now provide some sort of remote or virtual reference desk as well. See also **reference, reference librarian**; compare to **virtual reference**.

reference librarian. A type of librarian specializing in assisting you with any and every aspect of the research process. See also **reference, reference desk**; compare to **virtual reference**.

reference page. See **works cited**.

references. See **works cited**.

relative value. The value of one assignment relative to another. For example, your term paper might be worth 50 percent of your grade for a class. This means that it is worth as much as all other assignments combined. Compare to **inherent value**.

relevancy. A concept used in evaluating information that refers to the degree to which the information meets a specific information need. Compare to **accuracy, readability**.

reliability. A term typically associated with primary research that refers to the degree to which a test consistently measures whatever is being measured. Compare to **validity**.

research. Involves acquiring, interpreting, assimilating, and presenting information in a systematic and organized manner. Research provides a description, explanation, and deeper understanding of a particular topic, idea, problem, or set of facts.

research article. A specific type of article that reports the results of primary research. Research articles typically consist of five standard sections: an introduction; a review of the literature, methods, results, or findings; and discussion or conclusion.

research paper. See **term paper**.

research questions. Specific questions that you hope to answer through your research and that will form the basis for your overall paper. Research questions narrow your purpose statement into the fundamental questions inherent in your overall topic.

research time line. A sort of calendar on which you map your term paper by assigning proposed completion dates for each aspect of your research assignment.

rough draft. A version of your document completed before your final draft. You may (or may not) be asked to save and submit your rough drafts. Compare to **final draft**.

scholarly publications. Also called *academic publications*. Publications both written and presented at a scholarly or academic level. Because the information is typically produced by individuals working in a field or occupation related to the topic of the publication, the information tends to be more reliable than that in popular, consumer-level publications dealing with the same topic. All peer-reviewed publications are scholarly, but not all scholarly publications are peer-reviewed. Compare to **popular publications, peer-reviewed publications**.

school library. Associated with K–12 schools or school districts. It is learner-centered and typically contains books, periodicals, and various media (e.g., DVDs) for both educational and entertainment purposes. Compare to **academic library, public library, special library**.

search engine. A search tool used to locate information on the World Wide Web.

search history. A record of the terms, search limits, and strategies used in your searches and the results that were generated from such. See also **search tool**.

search limits. Also called *limits, limiters, filters*. Options used in searching that restrict your results to only information resources meeting certain other, non-subject-related criteria. Limiting options vary by database, but common options include limiting results to materials available full-text in the database, to scholarly publications, to materials written in a particular language, to materials available in a particular location, or to materials published at a specific time.

search syntax. The way you enter your search into a search tool.

search tool. A printed or electronic technology used to locate books, articles, and other sources of information. See also **search engine**; compare to **database, index**.

secondary research. Reports on, synthesizes, and interprets previously researched information and, as a result, is more subject to errors of interpretation, emphasis, memory, and personal bias. For example, you read and report on information you find in articles, books, and other sources about the ability of drug X to cure autism. Compare to **primary research**.

secondary source. Medium for presenting secondary research. Examples include books, biographies, histories (not autobiographical), magazine articles, and newspapers or news reports. Compare to **primary source**.

self-recycling. A type of plagiarism in which you use the same paper or project for multiple purposes. For example, you have two term papers due in the same semester. To save time and effort, you write one paper and submit it in both classes. See also **plagiarism, intentional plagiarism, unintentional plagiarism**.

skimming. A reading technique in which you read everything at a basic, surface level to determine whether the piece is relevant and worth reading in more detail later. Compare to **critical reading**.

source list. See **works cited**.

special library. Gears its resources and services to a specific topic (e.g., a particular president, business) or population (e.g., the blind) and may or may not be open to the public. Compare to **academic library, public library, school library**.

style guide. See **citation style manual**.

style manual. See **citation style manual**.

subject specialist. A librarian who has a graduate degree or extensive experience in a specific content area. As a result, such librarians may be better able to assist you if your research involves the subject of their specialization.

summarizing. A means of incorporating text into your paper by condensing original source material to present main ideas in a narrower, more focused way. Compare to **paraphrasing, quoting**.

term paper. Also called *research paper, capstone paper*. Typically a written report representing the final product of a semester-long (i.e., term) effort involving finding sources of information and analyzing and synthesizing them in a meaningful way to demonstrate your understanding of a topic or issue.

term paper mill. Also called *paper mill*. Refers to a business or service online and elsewhere that sells term papers or that has someone write one for you. Use of these papers is seen (at best) as cheating and will result in a failing grade or worse.

thesis statement. Also called *purpose statement*. A summary in one to two declarative sentences indicating what you hope to achieve through your research, typically including the perspective you plan to take on such.

truncation. Use of a character at the end of a string of text to find all variations. The * in *commun**, for example, would find commun*ism*, commun*al*, and commun*istic* but also commun*ication* and commun*ity*. Compare to **wildcard**.

ultrafiche. Ultrafiche content is reduced even farther than standard microfiche content. Ultrafiche is typically associated with oversized items such as newspapers and often requires its own lens or equipment to read and print. See also **microforms**; compare to **microfilm, microfiche, microcard**.

unified search tool. Search tool enabling researchers to search multiple search tools simultaneously.

unintentional plagiarism. A type of plagiarism committed accidentally and resulting from such factors as a lack of knowledge of proper source use, a misunderstanding of the rules of citation, or careless note taking. See also **plagiarism, intentional plagiarism, self-recycling**.

user education. See **instruction**.

validity. A term typically associated with primary research that essentially refers to the accuracy of the results. Compare to **reliability**.

virtual reference. A means of providing reference services remotely via the Web and communication software. Chat, e-mail, and videoconferencing software are often used to provide this service. Compare to **reference**.

wildcard. A symbol that takes the place of letters in a string of text. For example, instead of doing separate searches for *Brazil* and *Brasil*, entering *Bra?il* will find both spellings. Compare to **truncation**.

works cited. Also called *references, bibliography, source list.* A listing of the sources of information you used to write your paper, formatted in the appropriate or required citation style. It will usually be at the very end of your paper.

writing center. An agency on most campuses where you can get assistance with writing and editing all facets of your term paper and other writing assignments.

INDEX

grammar, 138, 159–160
Guided Search, PILOT, 175

H
hasty generalization, 134–135
help
    asking for, 16–18
    asking for help with search, 187–188
    asking for help with term paper, 167
    librarian, choice of, 44–45
    research help from reference librarian, 43–44
highlighting, 27–28
host, of website, 136
how-to organizing pattern, 162
hypothesis, 69–70

I
ideas, 25–26
ignorance, appeal to, 134
ILL (interlibrary loan), 41–42, 92, 78–79
images, 53, 110–111
immediacy, myth of, 114
impact words, 101
index
    description of, 75–76
    research function of, 85
    search for articles with, 87, 88
index cards, 29–30, 31
inexperience, research delays from, 21–22
information desk, 41
information formats, 81–83
    See also format
information resources
    access issues, 77–78
    date of information used in term paper, 52
    difficulty in finding, 73
    librarian knowledge of available
        resources, 43–44
    reasons students should go to library, 38–39
    reflections on, 79
    search for articles, 175–188
    search for books, 171–175
    search for websites, 188–192
    search tools, anatomy of, 76–77
    search tools, types of, 75–76
    source materials, 73–75
    unavailable, 78–79
information resources, accessing/acquiring
    articles, considerations before search, 86–87

articles, searching for, 87–90
books/monographs, 84–85
depth of content, 83–87
information formats, 81–83
interlibrary loan, 92
reflections on, 92
as second stage of research, 4–5
websites, 91
inherent value, 49–50
instruction, at academic library, 42
instructor
    asking for help from, 17
    asking for help/feedback from, 167
    assignment elements and, 50
    grading of assignment by, 49–50
    knowing when to ask for advice from, 12
    topic change, discussion with, 71, 111
intellectual property (IP), 141–142
intentional plagiarism, 151
interface, 3, 93–94
interlibrary loan (ILL), 41–42, 92, 78–79
Internet
    availability of information with, 37
    for finding articles, search tool vs., 86
    limitations of research with, 3–4
    locating e-versions of articles on, 118
    locating materials, 115
    search for websites, 188–192
    search results, 118–119
    search strategies for, 108–110
    websites, search engines for, 77
    See also Web (World Wide Web)
interpretations, different, 132
in-text citation, 147, 148
introduction
    description of, 11
    as element of term paper, 10
    in research article, 124
    use of different introductions in writing,
        163
IP (intellectual property), 141–142

J
jargon
    glossary of unfamiliar terms, 122
    readability and, 125
    of subject-specific resources, 84
    virtual reference assistance and, 46
    writing at appropriate level, 164

journal
    differences among types of periodicals,
        89–90
    locating articles, 117–118
    scholarly/academic information in, 56
    See also periodical

K

keyword searching
    as default search engine option, 91
    field searching vs., 94–98
    Internet searching by keyword only, 190
    overview of, 95
    search engine rankings and, 109
    for search for articles, 178, 180–181
    in search for websites, 188
    search strategies, reflections on, 111–112
    tips for, 96
    trying different search terms/keywords,
        100–104
    with unified search tool, 108

L

language, 189–190
    See also jargon; vocabulary
"last update" notification, 138
LC (Library of Congress) Classification
    scheme, 116
LCSH (Library of Congress Subject
    Headings), 98
learning, 1–2
legal issues. *See* ethical/legal issues
length, of term paper, 53
librarian
    of academic library, 41–42
    asking for help from, 17
    choice of, 44–45
    definition of, 42–43
    knowledge of, 44
    locating materials, 115–118
    reasons students should go to library, 38–39
    reference librarian, research help from,
        43–44
    reflections on, 46–47
    topic selection, help with, 71
library
    academic library, anatomy of, 41–42
    access issues, identifying/addressing, 19
    definition of, 37

history of, 37–38
interlibrary loan request, 92
library-based content, format of, 82
reasons students do not go to, 38
reasons students should go to, 38–39
reflections on, 46–47
types of, 39–41
virtual reference services, 45–46
website, access to indexes/other search
    tools on, 81
Library of Congress (LC) Classification
    scheme, 116
Library of Congress Subject Headings
    (LCSH), 98
library online catalog, 75, 171–175
limits, 105, 186, 191
links, 136
list of sources
    citation style guide, 149–150
    description of, 148
    function of, 147
    See also bibliography
literature review, 124

M

magazine, 89–90, 122–123
    See also periodical
main ideas, 25–26
mapping, 65–66
menu, of topics, 61
methodology, 124
microforms, 82
MLA (Modern Language Association)
    style, 52, 148, 149
monograph
    accessing/acquiring, 84–85
    locating, 115–117
    research function of, 85
    strengths/weaknesses of, 74
motivation, for reading for research, 122
multiple resources, searching
    simultaneously, 107–108
myths, 114

N

name-calling, 134
noise words, 101–102
nonresearchable topics, 62–63, 72
nontextual information, 110–111

notes
  citation-specific notes, 30–31
  developing method for, 27
  highlighting vs., 27–28
  note-taking strategies, 29–30
  style for, 150
  types of, 28–29

O

obligations, 22, 24
online public access catalog (OPAC), 75
open topic, 61
OR, Boolean operator, 106–107
organization, content, 136, 161–162
outline, of sources, 49
overwhelmed, feeling, 22

P

page limit, 53, 166
paper mills, 153
paraphrasing
  example of, 146
  incorporating text with, 145
  reflections on, 154–155
  summarizing vs., 146–147
patience, 99–100
peer-reviewed publications, 57
periodical
  differences among types of, 89–90
  locating articles, 117–118
  search for articles, 87–89
  search for articles, considerations before,
    86–87
  strengths/weaknesses of, 74
personal attack, 134
personal note, 28
perspective, 99, 104, 105
photograph, search for, 110–111
phrase searching, 107
physical access, 78
physical materials, 115
PILOT (online library catalog), 170,
    171–175
plagiarism
  characteristics of, 151
  citation to avoid, 143
  definition of, 142
  reasons to avoid, 151–152

term paper mills, 153
plagiarism-detection software, 152, 153
planning, 4, 19
  See also research preparation
popular publications, 56
popularity, appeal to, 134
post hoc fallacy, 134
predetermined topic, 61
present tense, 163
primary research, 8–9, 55, 123
primary source, 8, 55
print resources
  advantages/disadvantages of, 82
  information available only in, 3
  printed periodicals, shelving of, 117
  as search tools, 93
  See also books
printing, 19
problem/solution organizing pattern, 162
process, research, 6–8
pro/con organizing pattern, 161
procrastination, 21
professional credibility, 143
proofreading, 159–160, 165
protection of work, 167
public library, 40
publisher, of website, 136
purpose statement
  function of, 68
  generation of for search, 169
  impact words, examining for, 101
  instructions for drafting, 68–69
  organization of content and, 161
  relevancy of source material for, 126
  weak, rewriting, 72
  in writing process, 160
  See also thesis statement

Q

quality, 162–165
quantity, of sources, 54
questions, 43, 46
quotation marks, 107, 179
quoting
  example of, 146
  incorporating text with, 145
  reflections on, 154–155
  in term paper, instructions for, 164

R

ranking, search results, 118–119

readability, 125, 136

reading

    article content, evaluation of level of, 122–125

    challenges, 121–122

    for comprehension, 26–27

    critically, 26

    disagreement among sources, 131–133

    errors in reasoning, 133–135

    evaluation of what you read, 125–131

    focus, maintaining during, 18

    main ideas, grasping, 25–26

    reflections on, 35, 139

    for research, 121

    skimming, 24–25

reasoning, errors in, 133–135

records, database, 76–77

red herring, 133

refereed publications, 57

reference desk, 41

reference librarian

    at academic library, 41, 42

    research help from, 43–44

    research training of, 42–43

references, 11–12, 129

    See also bibliography

reflections

    on ethical/legal issues, 154–155

    on information resources, 79

    on information resources, accessing/acquiring, 92

    on reading/evaluation, 139

    on research, 14

    on research preparation, 34–36

    on search results, 119

    on search strategies, 111–112

    on topic, 71–72

    on writing your paper, 168

relationship, with librarian, 44–45

relative value, 50

relevancy, 114, 126–127

reliability, 130–131

remote access, 19, 78

removable storage device, 19, 167

research

    challenges of, xi

    continued research after initial search, 192–194

    defining, 1–2

    doing too much/too little, 12–13

    help from reference librarian, 43–44

    Internet, reasons not to use exclusively, 3–4

    letting topic guide research, 60

    nonresearchable topics, 62–63

    process, 6–8

    process, delays in, 21–22

    questions, 70

    reading for, 121–122

    reasons for doing research, 2–3

    reflections on, 14

    researchable topic, selection of, 61–62

    research-as-foreign-language metaphor, xii

    stages of, 4–5

    term paper, completion of, 12

    term paper, overview of, 8–12

    topic, focusing around, 68–70

research articles, 122, 123–125

(Re)Search Cycle, 7–8

research paper, 8–9

research preparation

    access issues, identifying/addressing, 19

    computer fluency, 32–34

    copy or print all sources, 31–32

    focus, maintaining, 18–19

    help, asking for, 16–18

    need for, 15

    notes, developing method for taking, 27–31

    reading strategies, adopting new, 24–27

    reflections on, 34–36

    research time line, 22–24

    skills for research, 15–16

    stress, acknowledging/managing, 19–20

    time management, 20–22

research time line, 22–24

research topic. *See* topic

research-as-foreign-language metaphor, xii

resources. *See* information resources

responsibility, 143

restricted access, 78

results/findings, 124

revision, of paper, 5